FORT SAM

THE STORY OF FORT SAM HOUSTON, TEXAS

Fort Sam

The Story of Fort Sam Houston, Texas

Eldon Cagle Jr.

MAVERICK PUBLISHING COMPANY

MAVERICK PUBLISHING COMPANY
P.O. Box 6355, San Antonio, Texas 78209

Library of Congress Cataloging-in-Publication Data

Cagle, Eldon–
    Fort Sam : the story of Fort Sam Houston, Texas / Eldon Cagle Jr.
          p. cm.
      Includes bibliographic references and index.
    ISBN 1-893271-24-2 (hardcover : alk. paper) — ISBN 1-893271-25-0 (pbk. :
    alk. paper)
    1. Fort Sam Houston (Tex.)—History. I. Title.
UA26.S3 C34 2002
355.7'09764'351—dc21
                                2002009568

First page: Top of the Quadrangle clocktower.
Frontispiece: The U.S. Army's Second Division, commanded by Brig. Gen. Paul B. Malone, formed a human version of the division insignia on Fort Sam Houston's parade ground in 1925. Formation design was by Lt. F. X. Dorn. *(Fort Sam Houston Museum)*

Contents

Major A MacArthur, Capt. R E Thompson, Capt. E S Dudley, Major C E Dutton, Lieut. J S Mallory, Lieut. G T Langhorne, Capt. F J Kernan, Major J F Weston, Lieut. J E Myers, Lieut. H L
Asst. Adjt. General. Chief Sig. Officer. Asst. Q. M. Chief Ord. Officer. Aide-de-Camp. Aide-de-Camp. Act. Judge Adv. Chief C. S. I. S. A. Practice. Act. Eng. O

Major P D Vroom, Colonel O M Terrell, General Frank Wheaton, Colonel J C Baily, Major G O Smith,
Inspector General. Chief Paymaster. Department Commander. Medical Director. Chief Quartermaster.

Brigadier General Frank Wheaton, Personal and Department Staff.

Department Headquarters, San Antonio, Texas, April II, 1894.

The Army's Southern Department headquarters staff at Fort Sam Houston in 1894 included Maj. Arthur MacArthur, far left, father of Gen. Douglas MacArthur, who was then attending West Texas Military Academy across the street. The officers gathered at the commander's home, now known as the Pershing House.

Foreword

I had the good fortune of commanding Fort Sam Houston, Texas. I lived in the magnificent Pershing House, had my office in the historic Quadrangle and walked the hallowed halls of what I consider to be America's most history-filled military post.

This unique book documents the history of a place we call simply Fort Sam. A place we often take for granted. A place many have heard of but know little about.

Fort Sam was once the largest post in the United States Army. It has witnessed westward expansion, preparation for world wars and military innovation. The old post in San Antonio has produced warriors, statesmen and heroes. Today it stands as the home of Army medicine and houses the headquarters of both the Fifth United States Army and the Southern Command. Fort Sam has served the nation well and continues to rank high as an Army symbol of excellence.

Fort Sam Houston is what I call a "beyond-the-battlefield" post, a monument that packages the history, tradition and memories to which soldiers cling. Within its stone walls and wrought iron fences is contained the spirit of the Army. That is why commanders at Fort Sam must always preserve the old buildings that echo the deeds and voices of past heroes.

Preservation of history and historic structures is not always popular. It often gets in the way of a commander's primary mission of training for, fighting and winning the nation's wars. Preservation does, however, deserve some priority on the mission list. The good commanders will find the dollars required for a balanced preservation program. They know it is the right thing to do.

Fort Sam has survived politics, neglect and base closure attempts. The old post could be up for grabs during the next round of base closures. If it is a Department of Defense candidate for closure, Army officials will have little recourse but to salute, remain quiet and hope for the best. It will be the fine citizens of San Antonio who take a stand to save the post.

If history repeats, Fort Sam will remain a national treasure. This telling of its story may very well aid the survival of this majestic landmark.

Tom Jaco
Lieutenant General
United States Army, Retired

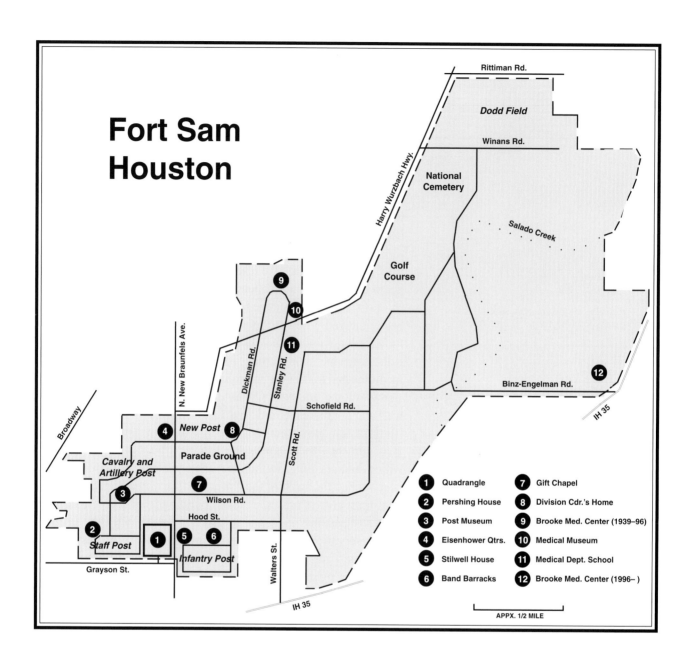

Fort Sam Houston

Rittiman Rd.

Dodd Field

Winans Rd.

Harry Wurzbach Hwy.

National Cemetery

Salado Creek

Golf Course

N. New Braunfels Ave.

Dickman Rd.

Stanley Rd.

⑨

⑩

⑪

Schofield Rd.

Scott Rd.

Binz-Engelman Rd.

⑫

IH 35

Broadway

④ *New Post* ⑧

Cavalry and Artillery Post

Parade Ground

③

⑦

Wilson Rd.

Hood St.

② ⑤ ⑥

Walters St.

Staff Post ①

Infantry Post

Grayson St.

IH 35

①	Quadrangle	⑦	Gift Chapel
②	Pershing House	⑧	Division Cdr.'s Home
③	Post Museum	⑨	Brooke Med. Center (1939–96)
④	Eisenhower Qtrs.	⑩	Medical Museum
⑤	Stilwell House	⑪	Medical Dept. School
⑥	Band Barracks	⑫	Brooke Med. Center (1996–)

APPX. 1/2 MILE

1. San Antonio Welcomes the U.S. Army—Twice

After Company G of Col. William Harney's Second Dragoon Regiment, U.S. Army, crossed the Cibolo on October 28, 1845, on the gently rolling green and yellow brushland below them the horse soldiers saw the lone steeple and clustered houses of their destination: San Antonio de Bexar.

There were still two months before the Republic of Texas would be formally annexed by the United States; it was December 29 when President James K. Polk signed the document admitting Texas as the twenty-eighth state. But in the eyes of the people of San Antonio, when Colonel Harney and his troops entered the village and passed through the dusty streets, their red and white guidons flying, they became Americans.

San Antonio had gone through a particularly difficult 40 years. Founded in 1718 as a waystation between Spanish missions on the Rio Grande and new ones in East Texas, San Antonio had attracted its own cluster of missions—five—and become the principal town in the Spanish province of Texas, with a population of about 3,000 by 1800. But repeated invasions and strife between Spaniards and Mexicans, then between Mexicans and Texans, had caused its population to dwindle to 800. Now there was hope for peace once again.

Harney's dragoons had been en route to San Antonio for more than six weeks. Leaving their post at Fort Washita, Arkansas Territory, they had reached Austin by October 10, in time for the statehood vote three days later. Of some 4,200 votes cast, nearly 4,000 were for annexation.

Statehood had been the ultimate goal for many of the Americans who settled in Mexican-ruled Texas with Stephen F. Austin at the invitation of the Mexican government in the 1820s. Between Nacogdoches, Waco and Coahuila lay an expanse larger than the original 13 colonies combined. West of Waco, Austin and San Antonio, real dominion was by neither Mexicans nor Anglos but by Comanches, the fiercest Indian horsemen to come out of the Great Plains.

The Mexican government saw the new settlers as a buffer against the Comanches. But when many of the colonists' rights were abrogated by a new Mexican dictator, Gen. Antonio Lopez de Santa Anna, the self-styled "Napoleon of the West," they rebelled.

So in 1836 when independence came—the cry "Remember the Alamo" still echoing from the battlefield of San Jacinto—leaders of the new Republic of Texas looked to the United States for a sign.

But the issue of Texas statehood was ensnared in the politics of the day. Since another southern state would strengthen pro-slavery

Sam Houston, who defeated Santa Anna at San Jacinto, became governor of the Republic of Texas, U.S. Senator from the new State of Texas and namesake of Fort Sam Houston.

Spain's military presence in San Antonio was based on Military Plaza, where the building erected in 1749 for the presidio captain has since become known as the Spanish Governor's Palace.

forces in Congress, northern politicians demurred. When newly planted East Texas cotton found a major market in England, causing even northern politicians to fear an English-controlled Republic of Texas on their doorstep, annexation of Texas as a new state gained broader support.

The formal transfer came in a brief ceremony in Austin on February 16, 1846. It was an emotion-packed and solemn occasion. As several hundred men and women gathered around the porch of the one-story, pine-timbered capitol, Anson Jones, the republic's last president, gave a brief farewell. The stars and stripes rose as the Lone Star fell, and James Pinckney Henderson, a North Carolinian, took the oath as governor.

Despite Santa Anna's signature on the 1836 treaty acknowledging Texas independence and setting the Rio Grande as its southern boundary, Santa Anna still viewed Texans as secessionists who should be brought back into Mexico, by force if necessary, and, despite the treaty, still believed its southern boundary should be farther north, at the Nueces River.

In anticipation of war, President Polk sent Zachary Taylor and a detachment of soldiers to Corpus Christi, at the mouth of the Nueces. They arrived in July. When Colonel Harney first rode into San Antonio, Taylor's troops had already been stationed on the Mexican "border" for four months. When Mexican officials refused to see the American emissary sent to discuss the matter, General Taylor was ordered to advance to the Rio Grande.

As residents of the largest town in Texas, and one a scant 150 miles north of the Rio Grande, San Antonio officials lost little time in seeking a permanent U.S. military post. On February 4, 1846, the city council offered the U.S. Army 100 acres at no cost near San Pedro Springs, just north of town.

Secretary of War Winfield Scott recommended to Taylor that the local commander, Colonel Harney, accept the offer. But Harney declined, believing the site too humid and unhealthy for the soldiers, and also difficult to defend from raiding Indians.

San Antonio's legacy as a military training center dates from 1846, when Gen. John Ellis Wool set up a training camp at San Pedro Springs for Mexican War volunteers.

San Antonio was picked as a training center for arriving troops. One group of 1,400 volunteers had been organized as the First and Second Illinois infantries under Gen. John Ellis Wool, commander of the Army of the Center, based in the Midwest. After a march from New Orleans they arrived in San Antonio in mid-August 1846 and set up their training camp at San Pedro Springs, on the land Colonel Harney had rejected for a permanent installation. Harney had just left on another mission—fighting unruly and fast-riding Comanches and Kiowas toward the Rio Grande.

Harney's dragoons were cavalry who were trained to fight mounted or on foot. Fortunately, he had permission to enlist the aid of "Texas troops"—settlers who had learned Indian fighting as a means of survival. Nevertheless, he returned at the end of the month with only a fraction of his men. He found spirits of San Antonians running high as soldiers and civilians alike talked of marching "into the enemy's country."

On September 21 a young Corps of Engineers officer, Capt. Robert E. Lee, arrived after a weeklong horseback ride from Port Lavaca. He thought San Antonio a "quaint border town . . . of about 2,000, chiefly farmers and herdsmen, many of them Mexican," plus 3,400 soldiers, two squadrons of cavalry, a battery of regular artillery, three companies of the Sixth Infantry and the two regiments from Illinois.

A Virginian by birth and breeding and a West Pointer by education, Lee would have the job of determining the best routes into Mexico, locating likely campsites, finding supplies, supervising road construction and building bridges, with the pontoons carried on wagons. When Captain Lee left on September 28 with General Wool's force—1,954 men and 1,112 wagonloads of supplies—it was his first combat operation.

In July 1848, the Treaty of Guadalupe Hidalgo ended the war between the United States and Mexico. In the settlement Mexico received $15 million and relief from debts. The United States obtained title to all the lands formerly controlled by Mexico: Texas—all the way to the Rio Grande—and present-day California, Nevada, New Mexico, Arizona, Utah, Wyoming and part of Colorado.

In early 1849 Gen. William J. Worth was commanding the region's Eighth Military Department headquarters, established in San Antonio two years before. With overcrowding acute, he split the San Antonio force into two camps. One was set up at a former Spanish mission—Concepción—south of town, the other at the headwaters of the San Antonio River on the present-day campus of the University of the Incarnate Word.

The San Antonio council, still trying for a permanent Army post, had offered the former Spanish army barracks on Military Plaza, but quarters were too few and the offer was declined.

At the edge of town, for storage Worth took over remains of the century-old Spanish mission church known as the Alamo. Severely damaged by the battle in 1836 and scavanged for building stones by nearby residents, it required $5,000 in repairs, including a roof.

In 1850 the Vance House, on the site of the Gunter Hotel, became headquarters for the Army's San Antonio-based Eighth District.

With the Alamo occupied, a dispute began between San Antonio and the Catholic Church over which was entitled to the rent. The resulting lawsuit was settled in favor of the church.

Then, in 1849, cholera struck, spread by the open-air water and sewage channels, the San Antonio River and interconnected irrigation ditches. Deaths averaged 25 per day. Estimates of the dead when the epidemic ended ranged from 1,000 to 2,000. Among them was General Worth.

Worth was succeeded in command by William Harney, by then a brigadier general. Late in 1849 Harney was in turn succeeded by Gen. Persifor Smith, who in 1850 established headquarters in a new two-story stone building on the site of the present-day Gunter Hotel. It was known as the Vance House after its builders, brothers John and William Vance.

The Vance House remained the Eighth District headquarters for the next 11 years, even though General Smith, in deteriorating health, on the advice of his physician moved with a detachment to the coastal town of Corpus Christi.

In 1850, San Antonio's civilian population was 3,488. By the close of the decade the population had more than doubled, to beyond 8,000, eclipsing Galveston to become again the largest city in the state. In the building boom and modernization, tallow candle lamps along the streets were replaced with kerosene lamps. An ice factory and a waxworks had come to town, as well as the first "real ice cream." Fruit trees and shade trees were planted to add color and soften the harsher setting of life in the Southwest in the mid-nineteenth century.

During this decade the Army's Eighth District had three main areas to protect: the Mexican border along the Rio Grande, the Indian frontier—roughly from Del Rio north to the Panhandle—and

On his first assignment to San Antonio, in 1846, Capt. Robert E. Lee found the place to be "a quaint border town."

the San Antonio-to-El Paso segment of the stagecoach route to southern California, its travelers being important contributors to the local economy. The chain of nearly two dozen outposts built in this region was supplied from San Antonio, in addition to support, on occasion, for Austin, Corpus Christi and the now-vanished port city of Indianola.

In 1856, an unusual military experiment brought an exotic display to San Antonio: camels and their Egyptian herders. Jefferson Davis, former senator from Mississippi, future president of the Confederacy and at this point secretary of war under President Franklin Pierce, sought to end the "Indian problem" and make the West safe for settlement. But the vast and often arid expanse of wilderness had no railroads or transportation systems capable of supplying frontier forts or even troops sent to pursue Indian raiding parties.

Figuring that if camels successfully carried supplies in the deserts of North Africa and Arabia they should also succeed in the slightly more hospitable reaches of the American Southwest, at Davis's direction the Army purchased camels along the North African coast. Accompanied by their drivers, 33 camels docked at Indianola in April 1856 and were driven inland to San Antonio, where they were corralled at San Pedro Springs. The camels became an instant sensation among San Antonians. They were soon moved out to more sequestered quarters at Camp Verde near Bandera.

Trial expeditions showed that camels could easily carry 600 pounds, traveled far without water and foraged easily. The camels, however, were difficult for American soldiers to handle, spooked horses and mules in Army camps and smelled bad, and the program was eventually abandoned. Some camels, released near Camp Verde, could be seen for years roaming the hills of West Texas. More than a few became supper for Indian families.

As Jefferson Davis's camels were nearing Texas, the new commander of the Second Cavalry was heading in the same direction. On March 6, 1856, the twentieth anniversary of the fall of the Alamo, Lt. Col. Robert E. Lee arrived again in San Antonio. Two weeks later he left for Fort Mason, 100 miles northwest, only to find that his soldiers had been reassigned to Camp Cooper, another 100 miles north.

Fort Mason's regimental commander, Col. Albert Sidney Johnston, sent Lee on to Camp Cooper, on the upper branch of the Brazos River. There the Virginian found only canvas tents amid rattlesnake-infested scrubland and occasional Comanche hunting parties. In the summer of 1857, temperatures in the shade reached 112.

The break came in July 1859, when Lee was sent to command the military post in San Antonio. He assumed command on the 29th, with offices in the Vance House. On August 1 he moved into his "river house," beside the San Antonio River at St. Mary's Street. But not wishing to be bothered with cooking his own meals, the new commander boarded at Mrs. Phillips' Hotel on Main Plaza.

Life in San Antonio was a welcome change. The close ties between the city and military required his attendance at dances and

A local militia accepted the surrender of federal troops in San Antonio in a ceremony on Main Plaza on February 16, 1861, 26 days before the fall of Fort Sumter formally sparked the Civil War.

other social functions. In 1859 he became a charter member of St. Mark's Episcopal Church.

A fellow officer describing Lee in Texas wrote: "With all his stern sense of duty, he attracted the love, admiration, and confidence of all. The little children always hailed his approach with glee—his sincerity, kindliness of nature, and cordial manners attracting their unreserved confidence."

But in October, Lee's father-in-law, G. W. P. Custis, died suddenly at Arlington, the family home overlooking the Potomac River near Washington, D.C. Lee's wife, alone and ailing, was trying to handle the estate's affairs.

As Douglas Southall Freeman recounted in his landmark biography, *R. E. Lee*, Lee went back to help but quickly found himself involved in one of the flashpoints that would ignite civil war: abolitionist John Brown's seizing of the federal arsenal at Harper's Ferry, up the Potomac from Arlington. Lee was assigned command of the detachment of marines that within three minutes stormed the arsenal's engine house, captured Brown and his men and freed their hostages.

Lee returned to San Antonio on February 19, 1860, to act as temporary commander of the Department of Texas in the absence of Gen. David E. Twiggs.

Lee found many of his soldiers deployed into Indian country to combat an offensive mounted by Comanches and Kiowas against outlying settlers. Residents around Camp Colorado had lost animals to the raiders; 63 mules and 3 horses were stolen from Camp Cooper, all mounts at the Indian Agency Office near Camp Cooper had been driven off and, at another fort, a civilian had been killed.

By mid-March the raiding parties had been chased back to the empty plains, and Lee could turn his attention south toward the Rio Grande border and Juan Cortinas.

For ten years Cortinas, a Mexican national, had been crossing the Rio Grande and assaulting villages along the banks: Eagle Pass, Del Rio, Laredo and Brownsville. Between raids Cortinas remained secreted in the canyons and valleys just south of the border, enjoying apparent immunity from the Mexican government as bitter feelings still simmered among the Mexican officials from Texas Republic days and the annexation by the United States.

Lee's troops spent two months chasing Cortinas and his raiders along the Rio Grande before getting things under control. He returned to San Antonio on May 17.

Now Lee looked forward to a peaceful and quiet summer, though he was becoming increasingly concerned about the darkening spirit spreading throughout the nation. When the November 1860 election brought victory to Abraham Lincoln, talk more and more turned toward secession. In a letter to his cousin Lee wrote from San Antonio: "One is rent by a thousand anxieties, and the mind . . . is worn and racked to pieces. . . . A divided heart I have too long had, and a divided life too long led."

On November 10, the South Carolina legislature called for a special session to consider secession. In Texas, the stars and stripes were lowered and the Lone Star flag from the days of the Republic was raised. Gov. Sam Houston, personally opposed to secession, was coerced into granting a special legislative meeting to discuss the question.

In San Antonio a secret secessionist society, the Knights of the Golden Circle, boasted of being able to raise, on a moment's notice, a fully equipped militia of 8,000 men. When local rancher Charles Anderson, whose brother commanded Union troops at Fort Sumter, South Carolina, spoke in favor of the Union he would have been mobbed had it not been for an opposing group singing "Yankee Doodle." James Newcomb's *Alamo Express* opposed secession. In May 1861 the newspaper office would be burned by the Knights of the Golden Circle, causing Newcomb to flee to Mexico. Anderson and others who opposed secession were also finding it necessary to leave quickly.

In mid-December 1860 General Twiggs returned to resume his command in San Antonio, and Lee went back to command Fort Mason. Twiggs, 70, a staunch states' rights advocate, feared retaliation from militant Texans if he were to put the Union Army in direct opposition and petitioned the War Department to be replaced. Word came back in mid-February that his replacement would be the First Infantry Commander, Col. C. A. Waite, a New Yorker and thus immediately suspected of being a hard-line, pro-union Yankee.

On February 1, the state legislature had voted 166 to 7 in favor of secession, making Texas the seventh state to officially choose to separate from the United States.

On the morning of February 16, Ben McCullough, along with some 350 men, took over San Antonio's Military Plaza, claiming it to be under Texan rule. Two days later Twiggs was to meet with

Texas Gov. Sam Houston opposed secession, but had to call a special meeting to consider it.

A major prize for the Confederacy was San Antonio's U.S. Arsenal, its headquarters the first permanent U.S. military building in Texas.

commissioners T. J. Devine, P. N. Luckett, and Samuel A. Maverick to outline with General Twiggs the surrender of Army property. Before the meeting could get under way, a detachment of the Knights of the Golden Circle seized the quartermaster depot at the Alamo. The sergeant in charge, William Edgar, sided with the Confederacy. Without a shot, the surrender was completed.

The U.S. Army's Department of Texas, its assets valued at $5 million, fell to Confederate forces 26 days before Fort Sumter was attacked in South Carolina, the official beginning of the Civil War.

A major prize was the U.S. Arsenal on the southern edge of town, between Flores Street and the San Antonio River, on a 16-acre tract purchased by the Army in 1858. Its two-story office building—which survives—was completed in 1860, the first permanent building built for the military in Texas. The arsenal vies with the old U.S. Customs House in Galveston as the first permanent U.S. government building in Texas.

Other property turned over included 1,800 mules; 500 wagons; 950 horses; 500 sets of harnesses; tools, wagon and horseshoing materials; 7,000 bushels of corn; clothing; commissary stores; and ordnance stores, all valued at $1.2 million.

For surrendering, General Twiggs was dismissed by the United States Army. Twiggs went home to Georgia and exchanged his Union stars for a Confederate Army general's command.

Lee, at Fort Mason, on February 12 received orders to proceed immediately to Washington to speak with the Army's commanding general. The next morning he was leaving Fort Mason when one of his young officers asked, "Colonel, do you intend to go South or remain North? I am very anxious to know what you propose doing."

Lee answered, "I shall never bear arms against the Union, but it may be necessary for me to carry a musket in defense of my native state, Virginia, in which case I shall not prove recreant to my duty."

Lee's stagecoach pulled up at the Vance House in San Antonio while armed Texans still held the Union officers captive. Recognizing the wife of one of the officers, Lee asked, "Who are these men?"

Soldiers from the Fourth Michigan, its band shown in San Antonio about 1866, were among the U.S. Army troops back after the Civil War.

"They are McCullough's," she replied, to Lee's dismay. "General Twiggs surrendered everything to the state this morning and we are all prisoners."

The Texans demanded a conference with Lee, who was offered command of soldiers and supplies just captured in trade for his allegiance to the southern cause. But Lee, holding his allegiance only to Virginia, which he still hoped would not leave the Union, would not side with what he reportedly called "a bunch of Texas rebels."

The Texans declared Lee a prisoner of war and held him under guard. They released him a short time later to continue his journey to Indianola and a ship east, but he was forced to leave his baggage behind as ransom. He never saw his belongings again.

No real battles occurred around San Antonio, as most pro-Unionists had departed and those of Mexican origin were not very concerned with a war based on a cause foreign to them.

But the city did serve an important supply function. Gunpowder made locally was stored in the arsenal's vaulted stone magazine, begun by the U.S. Army in 1860 and completed for the Confederate Army, which also finished an armory shop and built several frame buildings nearby. Women and young girls knitted clothes and underwear, wrapped bandages and made quilts. Gunpowder was made in the Alamo. Dances raised money for the cause and helped keep spirits high. After Gen. John Bankhead Magruder repelled Union forces at Galveston, a ball was given in his honor.

With distant forts no longer garrisoned, Indian raids on the frontier became more commonplace and some refugees moved to the safety of San Antonio. When the prospect of renewed U.S. Army protection came with the end of the Civil War in April 1865, the Army was once again welcomed into San Antonio, if not quite as enthusiastically as before.

2. From the Alamo to the Quadrangle

With the end of the Civil War, 4,600 U.S. Army soldiers were stationed in Texas, all under the Fifth District in San Antonio.

Those assigned to San Antonio found the reentry confusing. The district's headquarters was leasing offices in various buildings around town. The Alamo went back to serving as a quartermaster depot, but due to damage from a fire in 1861 extra storage space had to be rented nearby. The arsenal on Flores Street was reoccupied by the end of 1865, but funds for badly needed repairs did not come for several years.

Married officers and enlisted men with families fared well, living in houses rented by the Army. Infantry and cavalry troops, however, were billeted in converted warehouses beside the San Antonio River, the space cramped and poorly ventilated and having to be evacuated during high water in 1866 and 1869.

The Fourth Cavalry was camped along the river when it flooded in 1869. Almost overnight the polluted stream caused a cholera epidemic. Following heated arguments, the young medical officer, Dr. Redford Sharpe, convinced the staff that the solution was to move the entire unit out of the city at once, though the commander and others declared that evacuation would require weeks of planning and thus be useless.

After the Civil War the U.S. Army resumed using the Alamo as a quartermaster depot, supplying frontier forts by wagon until the moving to the new Fort Sam Houston in 1876.

Among locations of Army headquarters in San Antonio prior to establishment of Fort Sam Houston was the French Building, which stood across the street east of the site of the present Bexar County Courthouse.

San Antonio outmaneuvered Austin and New Braunfels to get a permanent military post.

But by the following evening, the entire Fourth Cavalry was relocated 13 miles away on the Medina River. The commander, ironically, was awarded a citation for the prompt action.

Aware of these difficulties and also of the economic benefit of keeping a strong military presence, municipal officials once again began seeking to get a permanent Army post established in San Antonio.

After learning that New Braunfels, 30 miles north, had offered the Army 150 acres at the headwaters of the Comal River as a permanent headquarters site, two San Antonio businessmen went to Baltimore, hoping to persuade railroad men to improve San Antonio's transportation facilities by extending the Buffalo Bayou, Brazos, & Colorado line to San Antonio. As further incentives, Alamo Plaza hotelier William Menger offered the government the lowest rents in town in new buildings he erected and Judge T. A. Paschal offered to give 20 acres adjoining the arsenal, though the Army declined the offer because the low-lying property was too near the river.

Then came word from Washington of a surprise move of Fifth District headquarters not to New Braunfels but to Austin, the state capital, 80 miles north of San Antonio. Under the command of Gen. Joshua Reynolds, the headquarters remained in Austin after Texas was formally readmitted to the Union in 1870. The Fifth District was reorganized as the U.S. Army Department of Texas, with Louisiana added. Fortunately for San Antonio, the quartermaster facilities and the arsenal were too well established to justify their removal.

The presence of these two facilities required a stop in San Antonio on the inspection tour of the quartermaster general of the Army, Gen. Montgomery C. Meigs. While in San Antonio, General Meigs was persuaded by city officials that while a new headquarters post was needed, it was economically advantageous to the government for it to be in San Antonio. Forty acres east of town, adjacent to the Army's corral for cavalry horses, was selected, and paperwork was begun to transfer title to the Army.

Meigs was back in Washington in May 1870 when he received word that the title transfer was complete. He notified General

After the Army moved its supply depot to Fort Sam Houston, the Alamo's interior framework for a second story was removed, but the roof the Army added, above, to the walls of the unfinished mission church remained until the 1920s.

Reynolds that $100,000 was allocated for a new headquarters and quartermaster depot in San Antonio. Meigs asked Reynolds to obtain suitable plans and forward them to Gen. Henry Halleck, commander of the Division of the South.

Lt. Col. James Elkin, new commander of San Antonio's depot, was ordered to draw designs for the post. Elkin's plan, a square compound 625 feet on each side, was sent to Halleck for approval. But thinking Elkin's structure too large and costly, Halleck reduced it to 500 feet per side. Meigs passed the altered plans and the opposing views of Halleck and Elkin on to Secretary of War W. W. Belknap for a final decision.

Belknap selected the smaller plans, and Meigs sent word to Reynolds to begin construction.

But upon arriving in San Antonio from Austin, General Reynolds would not accept title to the new property, stating that not only was the land donated by the city not the site that had been shown to and chosen by General Meigs, but it also had a 40-foot-wide ravine running through its entire length, rendering the property virtually useless to the Army.

By the time the city had purchased the correct site from the owners and given it to the Army with a clear title, it was June 1872. More than two years had passed without the $100,000 appropriation being used, and the funds had been returned to the national treasury. Getting the money back would not be easy.

Secretary Belknap was never in favor of the new post, and there were others in Washington who agreed. Gen. Phillip Sheridan, one of the Union's most famous generals during the Civil War and now lieutenant general of the Army, was one. He wrote the adjutant general flatly:

> The conditions of our frontier are being so rapidly changed by the progress of railroads that what may appear right and proper one year becomes, to some extent if not entirely, useless the next year. This is strikingly the case with the Depot at San Antonio, Texas. In a year or two, instead of wagoning supplies from Denison as now, they can go by the railroad now under construction to Fort Worth, on to the vicinity of all posts in northern or northwestern Texas, and the Depot at San Antonio would be only a good place for cobwebs.

General of the Army William Tecumsah Sherman thought the same.

Normally, such opinions at these levels would mean the end to a proposal. But by this time President U.S. Grant had sent his new budget to Congress; tucked in was $100,000 for San Antonio's new post. The budget passed.

When Secretary Belknap used his influence to squelch the San Antonio appropriation, the city turned to Thomas G. Williams.

An 1849 graduate of the United States Military Academy at West Point, Williams had married President John Tyler's niece and was in San Antonio when the Civil War broke out. Trading his lieutenant's bars for the rank of Confederate colonel, Williams was appointed assistant commissary general for the Confederacy. After the war he

The 3rd U.S. Field Artillery conducted this drill in the 1880s at the Army's new post in San Antonio.

returned to San Antonio to open a mercantile company with his partners, Col. John Winters and Gen. Frederick Steele.

As a former Confederate officer Williams was officially among the defeated, though he could list among his personal friends many influential members of Congress and, most important of all, President Grant. This made him San Antonio's best hope.

Williams reached Washington early in January 1873. On the 15th he met with Sherman and then with Meigs. Though he emphasized that the Army would soon spend more in rental fees than it would for the construction costs of a permanent post, he met with little success. He spoke with Secretary Belknap and again was discouraged.

Then Williams had a private meeting with President Grant, who had been unaware of the maneuvers by Belknap and others that led to removing San Antonio's funding from the budget.

Williams wrote San Antonio Mayor Francois Giraud that Grant "at once emphatically said that the withdrawal of the recommendation about San Antonio Depot was done without his knowledge or consent and that he would see about it at the cabinet meeting today, and he did so I am sure, for this morning I called upon Secy. War again and he was (much) more polite."

A new appropriations bill—the Sundry Civil Service Bill—passed Congress and on March 3, 1873, was penned into law by Grant. Williams, thinking the city's problems were at last at an end, wrote Mayor Giraud to declare victory. But Williams was wrong.

On March 24, in violation of the new law, Secretary of War Belknap ordered the quartermaster general to make no moves to establish the new depot. The order halted action for more than a year.

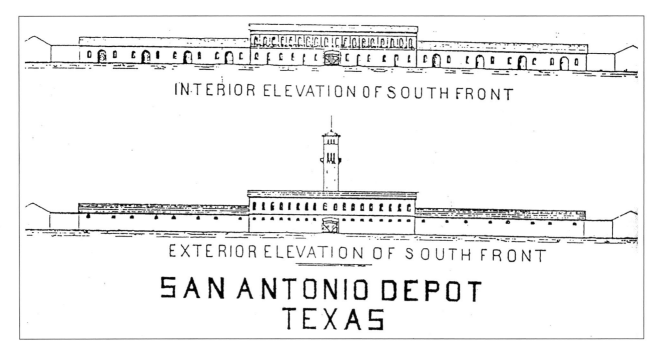

INTERIOR ELEVATION OF SOUTH FRONT

EXTERIOR ELEVATION OF SOUTH FRONT

SAN ANTONIO DEPOT
TEXAS

Plans for the new depot inside the Quadrangle originally included a second story over only part of the south wall. The second story was soon extended across the entire south front to accommodate all offices of the Department of Texas.

In May 1874, Thomas Williams again met with Grant, this time presenting him with a letter from the city stating that no action had occurred. In spite of the obviously illegal maneuvers by Belknap, the president showed little interest in San Antonio's plight. So Williams turned to the Texas delegation for help. Sen. James Glanagan accepted the challenge.

Senator Glanagan introduced yet another bill into Congress for the necessary funding. Although fiscal year 1875 was ending June 30, by March San Antonio still had no sign that anything would come of the new bill. On March 3 another ploy was tried—a petition with 496 citizens' signatures was sent to Belknap. An accompanying letter asked for the secretary's help and outlined how he had personally and repeatedly interfered with the law. Copies were sent to Congressman John Hancock and to Quartermaster General Meigs.

The petition worked.

On May 6 Belknap wrote to Hancock, explaining how he had had a change of heart and stating that the San Antonio post was, in fact, a very good idea. His recommendation was forwarded to Meigs.

While Secretary of War Belknap may have thought this ended the matter, it didn't. His actions in the episode were among reasons cited on March 2, 1876, when the House of Representatives unanimously voted to impeach him. Before the day was out, Belknap resigned.

On June 7, 1876, the Edward Braden Construction Company contracted with the Army to build the long-awaited post. Almost 30 years had passed—and San Antonio had grown nearly tenfold, to 20,000 people—since the city first proposed a permanent post.

But the new post would not be on either of the sites deeded to the Army in 1870 and 1872. The new commander of the Texas District, Gen. E. O. C. Ord, selected a site he thought more suitable by being

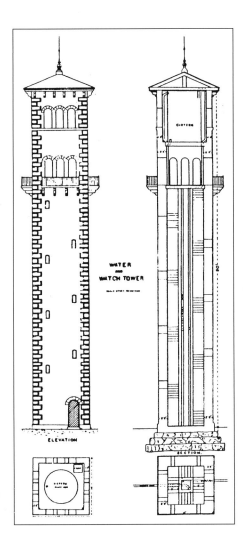

Army Quartermaster General Montgomery C. Meigs prevailed in his plans to enclose the post's water tank within a tower resembling one he had seen in Europe.

near a water source and not far from the proposed railroad station on Austin Street. So city officials transferred a third and final site to the Army: 93 acres just north of town on a brushy hilltop that became known as Government Hill.

The winning construction bid for the project was $83,900. Specifications apparently were either incomplete or vague because almost immediately construction ran into cost overruns, or, as they were called then, "extras." These amounted to 18 percent more than the original contract price and included privies ($138), a rainwater cistern ($2,141) and a signal lantern for the watchtower ($65).

Blueprints were also incomplete. Plans showing numerous buildings and stalls gave no detail of their intended use, an important point that would determine what interiors would require. Areas to be storage sheds, workshops and corrals for cavalry horses and mules—which would necessitate feed stalls and tack rooms—appeared only as unidentified individual squares, each 33 feet by 30 feet.

Among the planned structures was a watchtower, promoted as a lookout spot since the "Indian problem" was still fresh in the minds of many San Antonians. It was designed as a replica of one General Meigs had admired while traveling in Europe. He called it his "work of art."

In June 1875, shortly after the appropriations flap was settled, Meigs was succeeded as acting quartermaster general by Gen. Rufus Ingalls, a no-nonsense man when it came to fiscal matters. Ingalls thought the proposed tower overpriced and an unnecessary piece of European sculpture on the Texas frontier. He opted for a less expensive structure, "a tower similar to a lighthouse on a framework of iron piles."

Meigs, however, found out about the Ingalls plan and pointed out that he outranked Ingalls. Meigs's plan was adopted.

The Quadrangle neared completion as another event occurred, one that would not only end Army quartermasters' dependence on overland wagons to San Antonio but one that would end the relative isolation of San Antonio, the last major American town with no railroad access to the outside world. Shortly after 4 p.m. on February 19, 1877, the first train on the just finished Galveston, Harrisburg & San Antonio Rail Road arrived at the new station on Austin Street. That set off a two-day celebration the likes of which the city had never seen.

On board the 15-coach train were 800 "excursionists," guests of the railroad company from virtually every point along the line. Just outside San Antonio, at Marion, the train was met by a welcoming committee made up of the governor, lieutenant governor, attorney general, chief justice of the state supreme court and an assortment of lesser judges and dignitaries—including the superintendent of the insane asylum.

The Army had a featured presence at the event. Leading the torchlight parade from the Austin Street station just south of the still unfinished post down to Alamo Plaza were the Tenth Cavalry Band and

One of San Antonio's best-known landmarks is Fort Sam Houston's Quadrangle tower, shown rising above in 1876. Originally built as a water tower, in 1882 its upper rows of arches (far left) were partially covered by a clock (left) and later sealed entirely. Peaceful residents then as now have been deer, left, living within the Quadrangle's walls.

Soon after construction was completed the offices which at first extended only a short distance above either side of the sally port (below) were extended to house the headquarters of the Army's Department of Texas, recently returned to San Antonio after a brief stay in Austin.

Among support facilities originally within the Quadrangle were a blacksmith shop, above, and, below, a government printing office, shown in 1890.

a large cavalry contingent. Festivities continued the next day, which was also declared a citywide holiday.

Quartermasters moved their depot supplies from the Alamo into a Quadrangle not quite square, its walls built of limestone cut in the quarry that became Brackenridge Park's Sunken Gardens and hauled to Government Hill in wagons.

The Quadrangle's northern side was formed by a 624-foot long, one-story wall with storage rooms and shops facing inward where blacksmiths, carpenters and saddle makers could turn out harnesses, saddles and wagons. The east and west sides were inward-facing

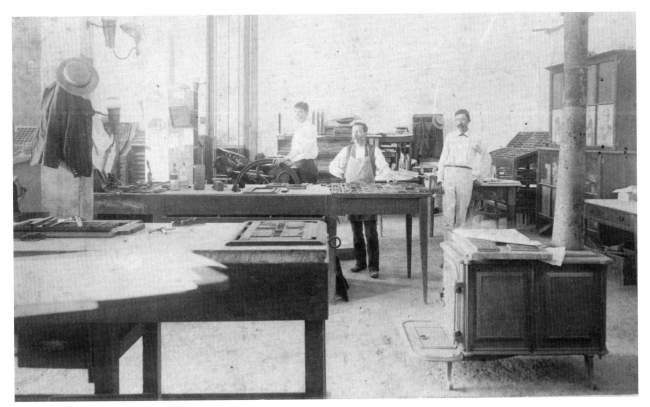

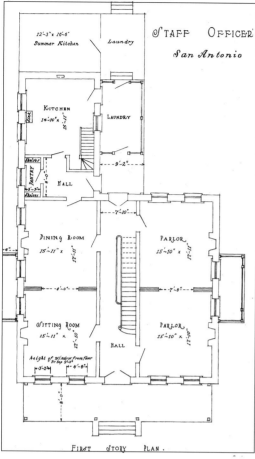

FIRST STORY PLAN.

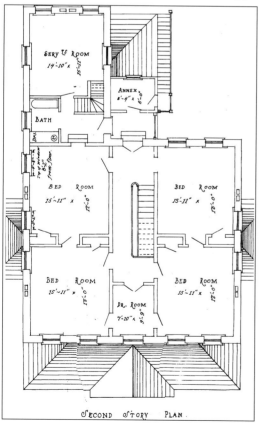

SECOND STORY PLAN.

buildings 499 and a half feet long, for storing such supplies as forage, commissary stores and uniforms.

The center of the long building forming the south wall, facing toward town, was pierced by a sally port, opening onto Grayson Street and large enough to accommodate wagons. It was the formal opening to the Quadrangle; two wrought iron gates were placed at the northeast and northwest corners. The sally port arched beneath a second story, yet to be extended the full length of the south side to accommodate all offices of the Department of Texas, which were waiting for construction to finish since returning from Austin to San Antonio in 1875.

Once the Quadrangle's additional offices were completed, on December 22, 1879, the headquarters of what was being called simply the "Post at San Antonio" moved in. A new telegraph line provided immediate communication with all other posts in the command. The refurbished arsenal at the southern edge of town was maintained as a separate entity and soon expanded.

The centerpiece of the Quadrangle was the square limestone block tower, at 87 feet the tallest structure in or around San Antonio. It offered an excellent view of the rolling countryside. Atop each side were two rows of arched windows, one row of three above another. With an internal system of pulleys and cables, the $65 signal lantern could be raised or lowered to light the entire compound for sentry duty. The tower also held a 6,400-gallon water tank that supplied the military compound until a large underground cistern for a pump-driven supply could built and filled.

In 1882, a four-sided Seth Thomas clock with a bell striking on the half hour was added, covering the top rows of arches. The bell was reportedly discovered on a gunboat that ran aground in Galveston harbor. It was brought to San Antonio to hang from an Alamo archway when the Alamo served as the quartermaster depot, then carried to the new watchtower.

Outside the new Quadrangle, troops lived in tents with wood frames and in frame barracks—to the delight of the post's medical officer, who had long sought better quarters for the troops on elevated ground.

In 1880 came plans for 15 officers' quarters along Staff Post Road, bordering the new parade grounds west of the Quadrangle. They were designed in an Italianate style then in vogue by noted San Antonio architect Alfred Giles. To the north were grazing fields for horses.

The first house on Staff Post Road was at the corner, the residence of the commander of the Department of Texas. It remains a magnificent two-story Victorian stone home, its original 10,830 square feet since expanded to more than 11,000 and including the kitchen, originally a separate building to the rear.

The home's external limestone block walls—topped by a copper roof and an iron-crested cupola—are more than a foot thick and enclose 11 rooms originally lit with gas chandeliers, a walnut and cherry central staircase, six and a half baths and eight fireplaces, six with

The first major development at Fort Sam Houston outside the Quadrangle was Staff Post (above, looking west from the Quadrangle's tower), designed bordering a parade ground in 1880.

Italianate style homes of cut limestone blocks were designed by San Antonio architect Alfred Giles in diminishing sizes for officers of field grade, staff (*plans, opposite page*) and company grade (below).

Grandest of all was the Commanding General's home, facing the corner of the parade ground, above. It is shown at right with Brig. Gen. David Stanley and his family, the longest residents (1884–92). The Stanleys' parlor is at lower right.

The Commanding General's home has since became known as the Pershing House in honor of its most famous resident, Gen. John J. Pershing, who lived in it just prior to being assigned to command Allied forces in World War I.

In 1886 the post got its first permanent hospital, now Sam Houston House.

A unique landmark on Infantry Post is the 1893 Band Barracks, with its third-story belvidere from which the band could play for drills and reviews on the parade ground below. Restored in 1996, it is the only building of its type in the Department of Defense inventory.

mantles of pink marble. The sweeping veranda with two-story tall white columns includes a gallery along the front.

Since its first resident, Brig. Gen. Christopher Augur, this has been the commander's residence. In 1959 it was named the Pershing House in honor of Gen. John J. "Black Jack" Pershing, who lived there while serving as Southern Department commander just prior to World War I.

As this was finished, 14 other officers' homes were added along Staff Post Road, of decreasing size and ornamentation for field grade and then for company grade officers. Line officers got termporary frame quarters along the parade ground's southeastern edge.

The temporary frame hospital built just west of Staff Post Road in 1879 was a welcome change from the only medical facility previously available to soldiers, a rented house that served as examining room, physician's office, medical ward, operating room and convalescent center. A permanent hospital came in 1886, a 12-bed facility built in the form of a "T." The central core served as office space with a second floor above. Wards extended to the left and right, with a kitchen in the back. As Sam Houston House, it now provides housing for important visitors.

The "Post at San Antonio" soon began to benefit from a nationwide consolidation of military forces. This was triggered by an unstable economy that required cost cutting, but it was made possible by the new stability following the end of the Indian wars and of post–Civil War Reconstruction in the South. But, complained Brig. Gen. David S. Stanley—Department of Texas commander from May 1884 to June 1892, the longest such tenure—to the *San Antonio Express*:

It is the disposition of the Secretary of War to abolish small posts and concentrate troops in large posts. I tried to convince the Secretary of the contrary, but I suppose the question of economy cuts too great a figure in the decision in this regard. The entire Mexican border is subject to outlawry. The Government will always keep posts at the points of entrance into Mexico like El Paso, Eagle Pass, Laredo and Brownsville.

To accommodate functions being consolidated in San Antonio, the Army purchased 43 acres east of the Quadrangle for the regimen

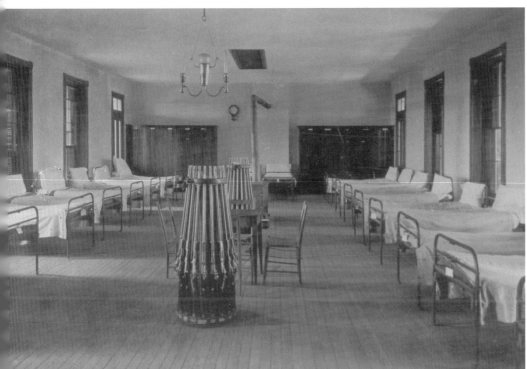

Infantry Post (top, south-east from the Quadrangle tower) included a Commander's House (top, left center), now the Stilwell House. Its long barracks with gun racks (left) featured a landmark sally port (above). Below, marksmen take a break during 1888 competition at the range near the present Winans Road.

Brig. Gen. David Stanley, commander of the Department of Texas from 1884 to 1892, in his Quadrangle office.

tal-size Infantry Post—originally called Upper Post, until the Infantry Post name gained use after World War I. Between 1885 and 1891, 60 buildings—most designed, like those on Staff Post, by architect Alfred Giles—were erected around a central parade ground. Two-storied, long brick buildings provided barracks, offices and storage areas for a host of different infantry, cavalry and artillery companies. Also built were a mess hall, hospital steward's quarters, gun shed and, along the northern edge of the compound, three cavalry sheds.

On the northern side of the parade grounds the unique 1893 Band Barracks Building was built, its third story a distinctive open, roofed belvedere where the band could play for drills and reviews on the parade grounds. Deteriorated and damaged by fire, it was restored in 1996 and is the only building of its type in the Department of Defense inventory.

In the center of the main Infantry Post building known as the Long Barracks was a sally port that became one of the best-known portals in the Army. The large open room above the sally port served as a band hall, then as a military prison.

Stationed at the fort for various lengths of time during this period were the 1st, 5th, 7th, 9th, 10th, 23rd, 24th, 25th and 26th Infantries, then the 2nd and 3rd Field Artilleries and the 3rd and 8th Cavalry Units.

Helping the quartermaster with supplies for the units were "two teamsters and one scavenger." Their pay totaled $100 per month, $30 for each teamster but, Quartermaster's Day Reports show, $40 for the scavenger since he provided his own horse.

3. Geronimo

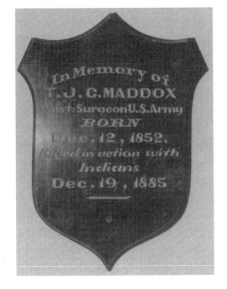

St. Paul's Episcopal Church, founded across Grayson Street from Fort Sam Houston in 1883, has this memorial to a victim of the Indian Wars.

Although the Fort Sam Houston quadrangle tower early on was considered a lookout for advancing Indians, such real danger to San Antonio had long passed. Military installations in the city could afford to be lightly defended; their commanders worried instead about the defense of forts farther west.

In the mid-nineteenth century, the western boundary of "civilized" Texas was essentially the 98th meridian, a north-south line just west of San Antonio. West of that north-south line was "Indian country," much of it desert or wilderness good for neither farming nor ranching. Beyond, a string of forts drew around them clusters of hardy settlers, who in many cases formed towns as market centers for the surrounding areas.

After General Twiggs surrendered the U.S. Army's 2,500-man force in Texas in 1861, the Confederacy considered other needs greater than garrisoning forts on a distant frontier. With those forts undefended, many settlers moved back east, while those who stayed found themselves exposed to sudden Indian raids and massacres.

After the U.S. Army returned to the frontier following the Civil War, in 1867 the Treaty of Medicine Lodge confined Indians to the lush grasslands of the Llano Estacado, centered in the Texas and Oklahoma panhandles, and promised that buffalo—central to Indians' physical and spiritual life—would no longer be hunted by the white man.

Yet white hunters still roamed the prairies, including the forbidden areas, slaughtering buffalo at will. In January 1871, a Kiowa raiding party set out for revenge. On the Salt Creek Prairie of North Texas the raiders came across a small wagon train with four men en route between Fort Griffin and Weatherford. All four died. Three months later came a series of Indian raids, scalpings and horse theft.

Texans accused the federal government not only of inadequately protecting settlements, but also of harboring Indians in the safety of the reservations to the north. As complaints and stories of tragedy continued filtering to Washington, General of the Army William T. Sherman came down for an inspection. With him were Maj. Gen. Randolph Marcy, a cadre of staff officers and 15 cavalrymen.

Their tour began in San Antonio, where the occasion of the general's visit was as much social as it was business. On April 29, a magnificent seated dinner for the visitors was hosted by lumberman J. H. Kampmann.

Sherman's party then traveled north to Fort Concho and on to Fort Griffin. But the general saw little sign that Indians even existed,

Apache captives led by Geronimo were brought from Arizona Territory to Fort Sam Houston by train in September 1886.

let alone that they were a problem. He wrote Adj. Gen. E. D. Townsend: "I have traveled more than 2,000 miles over what was Rebel Territory, and that without weapons or escort. I have received nothing but an excess of kindness and personal respect."

But General Marcy was more concerned. He had helped build the Butterfield Trail through the heart of Texas, the very road the inspection team was now taking, and was disturbed by changes he noticed along the route. Although Sherman at first discounted Marcy's fears, after reaching Fort Richardson his opinion abruptly changed.

On May 18, Sherman's party crossed the infamous Salt Creek Prairie and reached Fort Richardson at sundown. In a meeting with distraught pioneers General Sherman listened almost with disbelief as they described the violence they had experienced that spring and displayed scalps recovered from the attackers.

During the night Sherman spoke with Thomas Brazeal, who had just entered the fort, having been wounded in yet another Indian attack. To investigate his report, Sherman sent the trusted Col. Ranald

Geronimo remained a proud figure as he stood among fellow Apaches being held inside Fort Sam Houston's Quadrangle.

MacKenzie, a disciplined officer more at home in the saddle than behind a desk and whose service in the Civil War led Gen. U.S. Grant to call him—at the age of 24—"the most promising young officer in the Army."

MacKenzie's investigation supported Brazeal's story.

The next day Sherman's group unknowingly escaped an ambush that later the same day destroyed a train of 10 wagons, killing nearly all the occupants. MacKenzie, who attempted unsuccessfully to follow the war party's trail, rendezvoused with Sherman at Fort Sill.

For the next four years Sherman, by now a believer in the reality of the situation, presided from Washington over a campaign that finally, with the Battle of Palo Duro Canyon on September 28, 1874, crushed the power of the Plains Indians.

While the Indian wars in Texas may have ended, they continued elsewhere in the Southwest. In 1885 and 1886, in present-day Arizona and New Mexico, one of the bloodiest Indian campaigns ever was led by the chieftain Geronimo, who had sworn revenge for the slaughter of his family by Mexicans which he witnessed as a child. His band of Chiricahua Apache—about 150 men, women and children—raided and killed over an area of 80,000 square miles.

For 15 months the Eighth Cavalry joined in the pursuit of Geronimo's elusive Apaches, who were credited with more than 400 deaths, the majority Mexicans. Involved were as many as 5,000 Army troops, civilians and Indian scouts.

Finally, Geronimo and his tribe surrendered at Fort Bowie, Arizona Territory, following negotiations with the Sixth Cavalry's Lt. Charles Gatewood. The peace settlement called for transportation of

The Apache warrior Natchez stands at the right of the four captives photographed above before a Quadrangle wall. As the captives became a major attraction for San Antonians, Ahnandia posed at right with George Wretten.

three members of the band by train to Fort Pickens, Florida, where other members of the tribe had already been sent. The group included Geronimo's son, Chappa, and Cochise's son, Naiche, often known as Natchez.

The train arrived in San Antonio on September 10, 1886, amid a circus like atmosphere. Thousands of onlookers strained to see the famous Indian raiders, only to find the coach window curtains drawn, as the captives played cards in seclusion. Hucksters sold souvenirs. Arriving at the Quadrangle, Geronimo was welcomed by Gen. David Stanley. Fearing he might be executed, Geronimo was pleased to learn that his people were only being held prisoners.

The Indians lived in Army tents pitched inside the Quadrangle and were kept under constant surveillance, as much for their own protection as to prevent their escape. Unaccustomed to a city the size of San Antonio, the prisoners were frightened by the belltower—they thought it possessed by demons—and were amazed at the street-cars. They were ridiculed by white adults and stared at by children, making a lasting impression on those who watched them.

The friendly atmosphere in which the Apaches were kept did, however, also cause a minor public outcry. Thundered the *San Antonio Daily Light*:

> Are the military authorities afraid to mete out justice to the barbarian? Are they bound by conditions of surrender of which as yet the country has no knowledge? If Geronimo is merely a prisoner of war having been treated with and accepted by the government as such, the gravest of this offense rests with the government and not the Army officers.

Nohchlon holds her papoose as she stands with a friend in front of a tent pitched within the Quadrangle.

One business attempted to capitalize on the interest by advertising in the *Daily Express*:

These now very gentle two-legged brutes, it is hoped, will not escape the penalty meted out to white butchers of similar caliber. Should they, however, be sent to Florida to earn their own living in a civilized way, by cultivating the soil, the government should provide them with the CASSADAY PLOW—STANDARD CULTIVATORS—Available at Elmendorf & Co., Main and Alamo Plaza.

The Apaches were kept in the quadrangle for more than a month, while President Grover Cleveland decided whether to yield to demands that they be returned to Arizona for trial by local authorities or allowed to continue on to federal custody in Florida, as originally agreed.

Finally, Cleveland decided to honor the terms of surrender. When Geronimo's band left Fort Sam Houston for Fort Pickens on October 22, 1886, the Indian wars were over.

4. The Nation's Largest Army Post

Life in San Antonio in the 1880s resembled the "rapid transit" system in operation since 1875. "Rapid" meant that mule-drawn trolley cars could carry up to 15 passengers at the speed of five miles per hour, covering the two miles from Alamo Plaza to San Pedro Springs—including stops—in 25 minutes, in light traffic.

In town, soldiers at the Alamo Plaza bandstand could dance to waltzes or fast-paced polkas. Or they could charm local girls on post at band recitals daily at 4 p.m., or with the color of the frequent parades in full dress uniform.

The tempo quickened by 1890, as an international fair drew tourists from around the world and the last mule-drawn trolleys were replaced by electric trolley cars. Another significant event that year was replacement of the relatively anonymous designation "Post at San Antonio" with a new name: Fort Sam Houston.

In the early 20th century, military precision was often practiced in such parades as this Grand Review, which drew spectators to the edge of Fort Sam Houston's parade ground in 1906. The photo was taken by Chaplain Thomas Dickson.

In General Orders No. 99, issued by Acting Secretary of War L. A. Grant in Washington on September 11, 1890, it was declared that "by direction of the president, the military post at San Antonio, Texas, will hereafter be known and designated as Fort Sam Houston, in honor of General Sam Houston, Commander-in-Chief of the Army of the Republic of Texas, the first President of that Republic, and the first governor of Texas." But Washington didn't quite get things straight.

Sam Houston, whose victory over Santa Anna at San Jacinto in 1836 made him one of the best-known Texans of all time, was not the first but the second president of the Republic of Texas, serving from 1836 to 1838—and the fourth president, as well, serving from 1841 to 1844. David Burnet was the first. Nor was Sam Houston the first governor of the new state; that was J. Pinckney Henderson. Sam Houston was the eighth governor, serving from 1859 until he resigned in March 1861. He was also one of the state's first two U.S. Senators, serving from 1846 to 1859.

Sam Houston was an ideal naming choice at a time when memories of the Civil War still caused rancor between northerners and southerners. Virginia-born Sam Houston was respected by both, in the South for his record as a Texas patriot and in the North for his stand against secession, which led to his resignation as governor as civil war became imminent.

Brig. Gen. Joseph Duncan, commander of the Department of Texas from 1911 to 1913, is shown garbed in the General Officer's Full Dress Chapeau.

Another surname destined to be widely known also soon become associated with the post.

In October 1893, Maj. Arthur MacArthur Jr., Medal of Honor–winning hero of the Civil War Battle of Missionary Ridge, was transferred from Washington, D.C., to Fort Sam Houston. With him came his wife and his younger son, Douglas. Major MacArthur, whose additional heroism brought him the wartime rank of lieutenant colonel at the age of 19 and the nickname "Boy Colonel of the West" at war's end, was assigned to a Quadrangle office as an assistant adjutant general.

Son Douglas MacArthur entered West Texas Military Academy, later Texas Military Institute, then located across Grayson Street from the post. He graduated as cadet captain and valedictorian. He credited that education with giving him a good start as a soldier, a career that gave him his own Medal of Honor—the MacArthurs are the only father and son so honored—and ranged from a division commandership in World War I to superintendency of the U.S. Military Academy at West Point, five-star rank as Army commander in the Pacific in World War II and the post of supreme commander of United Nations Forces in Korea.

Shortly after his son's graduation in 1896, Arthur MacArthur, again a lieutenant colonel, was reassigned to St. Paul, Minnesota and the Department of the Dakotas, while his wife and son went home to Milwaukee.

Five years later, on February 15, 1898, the battleship Maine exploded in the harbor of Havana, in Spanish-controlled Cuba. Those eager to expand America's influence in the world seized upon the disaster as nothing less than the action of saboteurs bent on keeping the United States out of Cuba and continuing Spanish oppression of the Cuban people. Two months after that, Congress declared war on the once-grand Spanish Empire.

Already America's Gulf Coast was seen as a potential target. On March 16, an artillery battery at Fort Sam Houston was dispatched to Galveston to protect that port. A month later, with war declared, Fort Sam Houston's 18th Infantry was ordered out by rail to New Orleans and onto ships bound for Cuba. In the Pacific, the U.S. Navy was moving against Manila and the Spanish-held Philippines.

Heading for San Antonio at this time to organize his own type of fighting force was one of America's most colorful political figures—Theodore Roosevelt, 39, scion of a distinguished New York family, big game hunter, naturalist and, also, assistant secretary of the Navy.

Roosevelt had the idea of forming a unique type of cavalry regiment, one filled with a mix of hard-riding cowboys from the Indian Territory, gunfighters from Arizona, independent mountain men and members of New York's high society. They would form up in San Antonio and be supplied by Fort Sam Houston.

The press quickly nicknamed the outfit the "Cowboy Cavalry," or "Rough Riders," terms not always appreciated by the military. Complained one spokesman: "We are rather tired of hearing the regi-

In May 1898, the 1st Volunteer Cavalry—also known as the Rough Riders—set up a training camp on the International Exposition grounds south of downtown, where, below at far left, Col. Theodore Roosevelt relaxed beside Col. Leonard Wood, who later served as Army chief of staff during Roosevelt's presidency.

ment called a 'cowboys' regiment, an 'aggregate of rough riders' and so on. Its proper title is the First Regiment of United States Voluntary Cavalry and it is composed of men of tried courage and endurance and trained to the saddle."

Roosevelt succeeded in gathering a cross-section of colorful Americans of the time. One had been sheriff of Wyawiapi County, Arizona, another the western general manager of a life insurance company. Others were lawyers, ranchers, businessmen. One was a full-blooded Pawnee. A dozen Harvard College students left at mid-term to join. From New York's social scene came Woodbury Kane, a cousin of John Jacob Astor; Hamilton Fish Jr., son of a former secretary of state; and William Tiffany, heir to the jewelry company, who broke the code of ruggedness by complaining of "nauseating" food and accommodations. San Antonians were recruited in the bar of the Menger Hotel.

A *San Antonio Daily Express* writer described the group in the flowery verbiage of the time:

> Some of Roosevelt's Rough Riders came direct from the Plains of the wild and wooly West, and have more intimate acquaintance with the festive range cattle than with urban ways. Some of the others come from the polo, golf and lawn tennis grounds, from the college regatta course and from the fashionable drawing rooms of the East and are more acquainted with swell club life and dainty social functions than with the tented field.
>
> Yet these millionaires and sons of millionaires and the wild cowboys of the Plains are one homogeneous mass of patriotism and pluck, representing and illustrating our fierce democracy where every man is equally a sovereign and where crowns must be won before they are worn. Here the rough frontiersmen, daring but uncouth, and the cultured collegiate, genteel but full of spirit, stand upon a common level and mingle in a common purpose.

On May 7, 1898, the first troops of the "Cowboy Cavalry" arrived in San Antonio. Led by a noted Indian fighter, Maj. A. O. Brodie,

An artillery unit heads west down the parade ground in front of barracks of the Cavalry and Light Artillery Post, begun in 1904. The development included seven homes for noncommissioned officers, below.

200 Arizonans detrained at the Southern Pacific depot, then moved to temporary barracks at International Exposition Hall in Riverside Park south of town. Plans had been for the men to live in tents, but not enough were available. Officers, however, were furnished tents and expected to bed down outdoors.

Roosevelt was still in Washington, finishing Navy department duties. He put the new arrivals in charge of his friend Col. Leonard Wood, a surgeon who had received the Medal of Honor during the Civil War.

At Fort Sam Houston, Colonel Wood, a stickler for detail, took charge of procuring supplies. He found two train carloads of a new style cavalry saddle unacceptable and rejected them. Fatigues of brown canvas and hats squared in the front were chosen as uniforms. Machetes were picked over regulation cavalry sabers, and six-shooters and Krag-Jorgensen carbines were issued.

Roosevelt arrived in San Antonio with his valet on May 15, aboard the 7:30 a.m. Southern Pacific. Following a brief breakfast in the Menger Hotel dining room, he headed for his new quarters, a tent next to Colonel Wood's.

A competent horseman, though without previous military service, Lieutenant Colonel Roosevelt selected his mount personally, purchasing a "fine spirited bay" from a horse trader on St. Mary's Street. Never one to shun attention, he rode several times through growing crowds.

The May climate was generally "hot and dusty," one of the reasons San Antonio was chosen as the mustering point. Both Roosevelt and Wood believed the climate would help acclimate northern soldiers to the tropical weather they would face in the Cuban summer.

The daily routine was early reveille and early taps. Afternoon drills were long marches south of town, or close-order mounted drills to acquaint the horses—new ones were continually purchased by Fort Sam Houston's quartermaster—with cavalry discipline. Nor was discipline limited to horses. In one incident, a group visiting local saloons decided, Roosevelt wrote in *The Rough Riders*, "to paint San Antonia [*sic*] red. One was captured by the city authorities, and we had to leave him behind us in jail. The others we dealt with ourselves, in a way that prevented a repetition of occurrence."

Stables for horses and mules were included behind the main buildings of Cavalry and Light Artillery Post.

These fashionable units—which do not survive—were built on Infantry Post in 1895 as Fort Sam Houston's first permanent quarters for married enlisted men.

By the end of the month, Roosevelt believed the men—and horses—were sufficiently trained. On Sunday, May 29, the 800 Rough Riders broke camp at Riverside—since renamed Roosevelt—Park. Colonel Wood led the first three squadrons through town to the railroad depot, Roosevelt arriving with the remaining four at sundown.

By midnight, the 1,000 horses, 150 pack mules and supplies were loaded. But passenger cars did not arrive until dawn. Troops became scattered, and in the confusion and darkness, some, Roosevelt reported, "drifted off to the vile drinking-booths around the stockyards."

As the men left San Antonio for New Orleans and Cuba-bound ships, they left behind a ghost fort. Fort Sam Houston had a skeleton crew of 12: the quartermaster, post surgeon, and 10 soldiers.

Roosevelt's exploits with the Rough Riders, and their charge up Cuba's San Juan Hill, brought him worldwide fame. In less than a year, the war having ended, he was elected governor of New York. He was elected vice president 18 months after that, becoming in 1901, following the assassination of President William McKinley.

Victory in the Spanish-American War brought with it control of Spanish territories from Cuba to the Philippines, all needing to be garrisoned by a larger Army. Smaller units were consolidated at Fort Sam Houston and new recruits were added at Fort Sam Houston, already cramped for space and having to rent warehouse facilities in town as well as camping space for the 33rd U.S. Volunteer Infantry.

To carry out this major expansion, in 1903 and 1907 more than 470 adjacent acres were purchased to the north and east, and a "Cavalry and Light Artillery Addition" was added to accommodate a full cavalry regiment and a battalion of artillery. With the infantry regiment already stationed there, Fort Sam Houston became the largest Army post in the nation.

Design of the new Cavalry and Artillery posts would follow the Army's basic plan of combining new concepts with the existing style of a standard frontier post, with buildings laid out around a central parade ground. At Fort Sam Houston, no construction occurred at the eastern end of the parade ground to allow for future expansion.

A new station hospital with fully-equipped pharmacy was built in 1908. Within nine years the galleries had been enclosed and two wings were added.

Among temporary buildings added behind the new station hospital was the gymnasium of the "Physio-Therapy Department."

Construction began in 1904. Nine barracks, three for artillery soldiers and six for cavalry troops, were built of buff-colored brick along the southern edge of the parade grounds. Six cavalry barracks were of dark red brick and red tile roofs along both sides of what became North New Braunfels Avenue to the east and south. Each was of two stories with screened columned galleries and 10-foot ceilings for better ventilation in the South Texas summers. Each contained a company of troops, the artillery barracks slightly larger since artillery companies had more men. To the rear were lavatories and support buildings, including one mess hall for each pair of barracks.

Across the parade field, 41 two-story Georgian Revival–style homes were built of red or buff brick for captains and lieutenants. Each had three bedrooms, a servant's room and oak-finished dining rooms. A commander's home was twice as large. At the eastern edge of the cavalry barracks, seven smaller quarters were built in a similar style for noncommissioned officers.

A new regional Station Hospital was built in 1908 at the northwest corner of the post to serve not just Fort Sam Houston but also

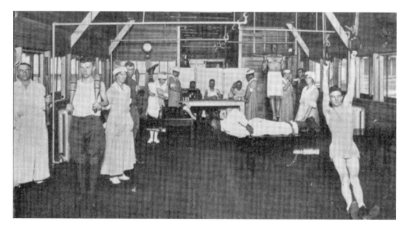

A 17,000-acre area 26 miles northwest of Fort Sam Houston was purchased beginning in 1906 for the Leon Springs Military Reservation, which offered vast isolated areas for maneuvers and formal military reviews.

smaller posts in the state. Its capacity of 84 beds was expanded two years later to 152, with construction of two wings. Soon after it was renamed Base Hospital No.1 in 1915, 50 temporary frame ward buildings were built nearby, putting total capacity at 1,000 beds.

With all the attention to the physical needs of the soldiers, Post Chaplain Thomas J. Dickson believed some attention should be given to spiritual needs, too. To serve Fort Sam Houston, in 1883 St. Paul's Episcopal Church had been built on Grayson Street across from the Staff Post parade grounds, but there were no government funds for a nondenominational chapel on post.

In 1907 Chaplain Dickson set about to raise private funds to build one.

Some $50,000 was contributed by civilians and post personnel for the new chapel, leading it to be named "Gift Chapel." The site picked was just east of Cavalry Post in what had been Maverick Park, since that parcel was purchased from the Maverick family in 1907. It was designed by local church architect Leo M. J. Dielmann in neo

Leon Springs Military Reservation offered an ideal location for training with new field artillery that had ranges exceeding territorial limits of Fort Sam Houston.

Thousands of spectators flocked to Fort Sam Houston in October 1908 for the dedication of the post's nearly completed Gift Chapel.

classical style, with classic columns at the entrance and a copper-covered dome.

On October 17–18, 1909, the nearly finished Gift Chapel was dedicated by none other than President William Howard Taft in an event featuring a military review with thousands of spectators.

Completion of the chapel's interior would take more years and more gifts. Stained-glass windows were given in honor of various chaplains and of Mrs. Fannie Easterbrook, wife of Chief of Chaplain Edmund P. Easterbrook. A chapel guild organized by Chaplain Ora Cohee in 1931 began raising funds for carpeting, lights, a piano and a cross. The organ installed during World War I in Camp Travis's Liberty Theatre was reinstalled in the Gift Chapel and replaced in 1969 with a new organ, to which two years later was added—with the aid of a major donation from Mrs. Dwight D. Eisenhower—the Eisenhower chimes. Flags of the nation's states and territories and those of units at the post were added beginning in 1971.

Most of the new construction ended by 1913. The numerous other improvements included paved streets and sidewalks, new mess halls for the Infantry Post, a veterinary hospital on Staff Post for the increasing numbers of horses and mules, stables, guard houses, new water wells, an ice plant, a telephone exchange building and, on the drill grounds east of the parade field, a gambrel-roofed radio station building—that survives—and two antenna towers.

By this point, Fort Sam Houston supported more than 3,000 persons and the monthly payroll exceeded $50,000. The next largest monthly expense was forage for the 1,000 cavalry and artillery horses, the single greatest source of income for San Antonio suppliers.

Horses as well as soldiers were getting field training in extended "hikes" into the Texas countryside. During the summer of 1900, the march of the third Field Artillery's Battery K some 65 miles northwest of San Antonio to Kerrville played an inadvertent role in influencing military history.

While en route, two second lieutenants, William Cruikshank and William Westervelt, stopped at Kerrville's St. Charles Hotel. Work-

President William Howard Taft offically laid the cornerstone at the dedication of Fort Sam Houston's Gift Chapel.

ing there was a boy named Chester Nimitz, 15. The three visited. Nimitz was impressed that the two were hardly older than he and that, as West Point graduates, they seemed to have a bright future.

On the basis of their conversation, Nimitz applied to Congressman James Slayden for an appointment to West Point. Slayden explained that there were many requests ahead of his, but there was an opening from his district for an appointment to the U.S. Naval Academy in Annapolis. Nimitz seized the opportunity, took a year of preparatory study and entered the Naval Academy in the fall of 1901. Four decades later Chester Nimitz would be an admiral of the fleet, the Navy's commander in the Pacific during World War II.

Growth of Fort Sam Houston was occurring as improved weaponry extended the range of rifles, carbines and artillery beyond what could be safely fired at the post. In 1906, the Army began purchasing land for artillery practice and as a permanent maneuver site beyond Leon Springs, 26 miles northwest of Fort Sam Houston. Within a year more than 17,000 acres of hilly brushland had been acquired to become the Leon Springs Military Reservation, with its own set of frame barracks and support buildings.

Regular marches—out what is still known, in part, as Military Highway—through the countryside from Fort Sam Houston to Leon Springs itself provided field training for the post's growing numbers of infantry, cavalry, signal and hospital units.

5. Making Aviation History

Aboard a souuthbound train, on the morning of February 5, 1910, the entire United States Army pilot corps arrived in San Antonio in the person of Lt. Benjamin Foulois.

The 30-year-old pilot's plane—U.S. Army Aeroplane Number 1—arrived shortly afterward, unassembled, in 17 crates—an assortment of pipes, linen, wooden struts, bamboo and baling wire.

Lieutenant Foulois had extensive flight training for the time: one cross-country acceptance flight of the airplane and 54 minutes of training by Wilbur and Orville Wright. America's first military flights had been made at Fort Myers, Virginia, but Foulois was being reassigned by the Signal Corps because of the more favorable flying conditions of South Texas.

The Army had purchased a Wright Model 1909-A biplane nicknamed the Flyer, which had crashed on September 17, 1908, severely injuring Orville Wright and killing Lt. Thomas E. Selfridge, the first American to die in an airplane crash.

While Foulois struck less than the classic pose of a military hero (5 feet 5 inches, 130 pounds), he had both military experience—he served during the Spanish-American War and saw combat during the Philippine Insurrection of 1899—and flight experience. He had volunteered for dirigible training, but he quickly saw the feasibility of using airplanes in reconnaissance patrol, air-to-air combat and aerial bombing.

Foulois's developing friendship with Brig. Gen. James Allen, Army Signal Corps commander and an early proponent of military aircraft, along with his contacts with the Wright brothers led General Allen to send Foulois and the plane to Fort Sam Houston, with plenty of spare parts. Continuing apprenticeship with the Wright brothers

This snapshot of Lt. Benjamin Foulois landing on the parade ground on March 2, 1910, after his first public flight at Fort Sam Houston, was taken by a spectator, C.C. Wurzbach.

WITTE MUSEUM, SAN ANTONIO, TEXAS

Test flights in the Wright Model 1909-A biplane were common during the Maneuver Camp at Fort Sam Houston in early 1911.

through correspondence, he trained himself. Years later, as a retired brigadier general, Foulois wrote that he was the only person to learn to fly by correspondence.

To become airborne, the Wright Model 1909-A biplane originally had to be launched by a catapult system of steel monorail, cables and pulleys. Moving the catapult required the ground crew to turn the ramp into the wind. The craft landed on a pair of steel skids that scudded along the ground, requiring the pilot to turn off the engine before touching down so the propeller would not break and cause the fuselage to be driven into the ground. Thus each landing was truly a crash-landing, beginning the notion that any landing a pilot could walk away from was a good one.

The first public demonstration of the aircraft in San Antonio came on March 2, 1910, a day late due to catapult system difficulties. As 200 spectators watched in an early morning breeze, Foulois's plane lifted off at the eastern end of the parade ground, not far from the "aerodrome" of one hangar and a few tents. He soared around the field six times and landed after barely missing an approaching car. Flight time: seven and a half minutes. Altitude: 150 feet.

Foulois repeated the flight three more times that day, crashing badly on the last landing. The plane was removed to its hangar for repairs.

A routine had begun: launch the plane, fly it, crash-land it, repair it, write the Wright brothers for help. As Foulois recounted these days in his autobiographical *From the Wright Brothers to the Astronauts*, he spent more time writing to his mentors back east than he spent in the air.

To make an impression on soldiers less than enthusiastic about Army airpower, Foulois buzzed their tents in a predawn "air raid." One of the least amused was his immediate superior in the Signal Corps, Major Squier, whom he had routed from the latrine.

In early 1911, the field Foulois used for flight practice was edged by a row of tents occupied by Corps of Engineers staff officers there

Lt. Benjamin Foulois, who at Fort Sam
Houston made the first military flight in Texas,
rose to the rank of major general.

for maneuvers. On one occasion Foulois made a low, wide pass, turned and cut his engine for the landing only to discover that he was landing short. In the direct line of his falling aircraft was the row of officers' tents.

Turning sharply to miss the tents, Foulois brought the airplane down directly in front of a horse and buggy. The frightened horse bolted, wrecking the buggy and slightly injuring the driver—the post's civilian newspaper distributor—as Foulois crash-landed nearby.

As the plane was being returned to the hangar for the latest round of repairs, the newspaper distributor unleashed a verbal assault on Foulois. Foulois turned toward a captain watching from a nearby tent and saw it was an old friend from his days at Fort Leavenworth, Kansas—Douglas MacArthur. MacArthur sided with the young pilot. Foulois realized long after that had he crashed into MacArthur's tent, world history could have been changed.

For the flying Connecticut Yankee, these were heady times of trial and innovation. Each new challenge was a first. If the airplane was taken to a height he had never reached, that was a new record. Or if he flew longer or made better moves, they were firsts, too.

Since his plane would "buck like a wild bronco" in the gusting winds of the Texas spring, Foulois sought to keep from being thrown from the craft. He visited the post's cavalry saddle shop, enlisted the aid of the leathersmith and designed the first airplane safety belt from a saddle strap.

As enthusiasm for flight spread across the country, one person wealthy enough to own his own plane was Robert F. Collier, owner of the popular magazine *Collier's Weekly*. Collier, who became one of airpower's most ardent supporters, purchased a 1910-B Model Wright biplane and loaned it to the Army until the government could see its way clear to buying others.

Collier's plane arrived at Fort Sam Houston on February 21, 1911, along with Phillip Parmalee, Collier's newly trained pilot. Parmalee instructed Foulois in the latest advances in the Wright brothers' design. Old Number 1 was returned for repairs to the Wrights' factory in Dayton, Ohio. It ended up in the Smithsonian Institution.

In late February 1911, Foulois and Parmalee were sent by train with their plane to join infantrymen on maneuvers along the Mexican border. On March 3, 1911, their two-hours-and-ten-minute flight between Laredo and Eagle Pass became the first official military reconnaissance flight in history, though they saw nothing but sagebrush.

On the return flight, Parmalee accidentally hit the cutoff cord, stopping the engine. The plane crashed into the Rio Grande 25 miles from Eagle Pass. A nearby cowboy came to their rescue and rode into town for help. The embarrassed pilots took the train back to Fort Sam Houston.

In another effort to prove the importance of air power, on March 17 Foulois and Parmalee flew a message from General Carter, Fort Sam Houston commander, to Major Squier at the Leon Springs Mili-

At the Fort Sam Houston hangar in the summer of 1910, two enlisted men sit at the controls of Army Aeroplane No. 1, now in the Smithsonian Institution's National Air and Space Museum in Washington, D.C.

tary Reservation. The round trip took an hour and 45 minutes and showed that airplanes could circumvent shortcomings of radio communication and ground couriers.

On the same day that Foulois and Parmalee were reconnoitering between Laredo and Eagle Pass, Congress appropriated $125,000 for "aeronautics," to be spent on additional airplanes, pilot training and research, training a pilot corps, and additional airplanes. The bill passed through the direct lobbying efforts of General Allen, the Signal Corps commander who had sent Foulois to Fort Sam Houston. Allen immediately spent $25,000 on five new airplanes—three Wright biplanes and two "Type IV, Military" aircraft built by Glenn Curtiss's Curtiss Company in Hammondsport, New York.

Curtiss had established the first pilot training school in Hammondsport in 1909 and in the winter of 1910–11 opened a second in San Diego, California, inviting the military to send any officers they felt would make good pilots. Four lieutenants were chosen: Theodore G. Ellyson from the Navy and Paul W. Beck, George E. M. Kelly and John C. Walker from the Army.

After two months of training, the four new Army pilots joined Foulois in San Antonio. On April 5 Major Squier formed the Provisional Aero Company. Command went to Lieutenant Beck, who outranked Foulois. Rivalry between the two began. While waiting for the new planes to arrive, Foulois wrote the official guidelines and company rules.

The first aircraft to arrive was a Curtiss, designated U.S. Army Aeroplane Number 2 and assigned to Beck, who declared it superior to Foulois's Wright B. To settle the question, demonstration flights of each craft were planned. Foreign dignitaries were invited to observe, including military representatives from Germany and Japan.

Foulois and Parmalee's replacement, Frank Coffyn, performed their maneuvers, including a one-and-a-half-hour flight to be per-

After the fatal crash of Lt. George E. M. Kelly, further flights at Fort Sam Houston were banned.

formed "regardless of weather conditions." Foulois and Coffyn flew within the time limit in a steady rain, the first flight made in the rain.

Lt. John Walker was the first of the Curtiss trainees to fly. After a few minutes of aerial display he brought his plane in, landing so hard it unsettled him. Walker resigned from the Aero Company and never flew again.

The next day Lt. Beck took the Curtiss into the air and hedge-hopped mesquite trees and brush, but the engine failed and he crashed, uninjured. During repairs, Foulois for the first time saw the plane's internal structure. He warned Beck about a faulty piece of wood called the seat fork, which Foulois said was weakened by having been drilled through unnecessarily by the manufacturer. Beck ignored him.

On May 10, Lieutenant Kelly took off in the Curtiss for the first time. On his landing attempt he came in steeply, bounced severely, and made a second pass. On the final approach the plane leapt 30 feet into the air and headed for a line of 11th Infantry tents. Kelly turned to avoid them, only to stall and crash. He died a few hours later from head injuries, the nation's first on-duty death of a pilot.

Major Squier called for an investigation. Foulois, asked to serve on the review board, told Squier of his prejudice based on the incident with Beck and was excused from testifying.

The final report stated that Lieutenant Kelly "had made a not abnormally hard landing. Upon landing at least one and possibly both sides of [the] seat fork were broken at a point between pilot and footrest. At the same time it appears that one diagonal bamboo brace from the front wheel to front elevator was broken, and its mate bent.

"It is the unanimous opinion of the Board that the front wheel must have struck an abrupt depression in the ground or some obstacle causing the strain, which resulted in the break," putting undue strain on the controls when Kelly turned to avoid the tents—a landing site the board said that in any event he should not have chosen.

After the crash, General Carter prohibited further flights from the field—the aircraft also startled horses—and the Provisional Aero Company disbanded. Aviation personnel and equipment were sent to College Park, Maryland, where the Army was establishing a new flight school. The pilots' commander would again be Lieutenant Beck. Because of his conflict with Beck, Foulois was sent instead to the War Department's Division of Militia Affairs in Washington.

6. War on the Mexican Border

Not everyone in San Antonio in 1910 was as visible as Lt. Benjamin Foulois, soaring and dipping in his biplane. Below, in downtown San Antonio, a revolution was simmering.

In secret meetings throughout the city a group led by Mexican exile Francisco I. Madero plotted the overthrow of Mexican dictator Porfirio Diaz, and stockpiled guns, ammunition and supplies to outfit a raid into Mexico.

Unrest was spreading within Mexico itself, fanned by revolutionary rivals including Venustiano Carranza, southern Mexico guerilla leader Emiliano Zapata, northern Mexico Yaqui Indian leader Alvaro Obregon and Francisco "Pancho" Villa, a guerilla leader in the Chihuahuan Hills of northern Mexico. In November 1910, following the overthrow of Diaz, Madero succeeded in being elected president of Mexico, only to be assassinated 15 months later.

The Mexican border was scarcely 150 miles from San Antonio. President Woodrow Wilson believed it necessary to prove that America could keep unrest in Mexico from spilling across the Rio Grande and even that Mexico could be invaded if necessary.

In early 1911, some 12,000 troops—the largest peacetime gathering of Army personnel and equipment yet in the nation's history—assembled at Fort Sam Houston. A provisional division was formed in a Maneuver Camp east of the main parade ground. Commanded by Maj. Gen. W. H. Carter, it included six infantry regiments, an artillery regiment, a battalion of engineers, two signal companies—with five aircraft—and an ambulance company.

The Army was also sorting out the administrative role of Fort Sam Houston. In mid-1911 its Texas Department headquarters was moved to Chicago and merged with the Army's Central Department.

As local suppliers met the needs of increasing numbers of troops at Fort Sam Houston, a train of wagons from Pioneer Flour Mills paused outside the Quadrangle as it fulfilled part of a contract for a half million pounds of flour.

As unrest heightened on the Mexican border, in 1911 America's largest peacetime gathering yet of troops and equipment arrived by train at a maneuver camp that spread across the horizon at Fort Sam Houston. Above, it attracted the ice cream vendor and wagon at left foreground, as well as a crowd to watch the parade beyond.

Once detraining, left, and pitching their tents, below, the 12,000 soldiers settled down to such routines, right, as getting vaccinations, shaves, practicing with new machine guns and dining—on the ground. At bottom far right, the 10th Infantry stands at attention during a review.

Participants in the Maneuver Camp included at least 16 future generals in World Wars I and II, including Douglas MacArthur and George C. Marshall.

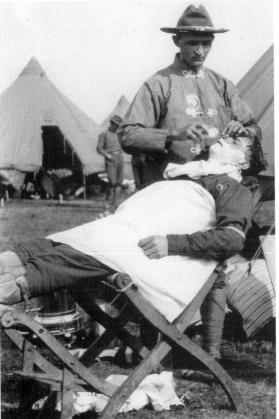

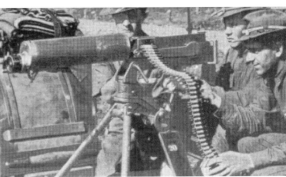

Texas Governor Oscar Colquitt and his staff came down from Austin to be honored by Maneuver Camp officers—all colonels or above—at this dinner at San Antonio's St. Anthony Hotel. The table, 75 feet in circumference, had a vast centerpiece of green forming a Lone Star plus decorations featuring various branches of the Army, with haversacks as nut holders and "heavy artillery" made by the St. Anthony's pastry chefs.

moved to Chicago and merged with the Army's Central Department. But logistics proved too cumbersome, the consolidation attempt was scrubbed and on February 15, 1913, the Texas Department was reestablished, with headquarters at Fort Sam Houston—apart from Southern Department headquarters, newly moved to Fort Sam Houston.

Still the situation in Mexico worsened, even as separate clouds of war began building over Europe. American-owned oil and mining operations in Mexico were seized by the Mexican government, American lives were threatened and in April 1914 American sailors were arrested and imprisoned in Tampico. In retaliation, the U.S. Navy bombarded the Mexican coastal port of Vera Cruz and took control of the city.

To improve Fort Sam Houston's ability to respond with ground forces, that same month Fort Sam Houston was upgraded to the status of General Depot. No longer would many supplies have to be shipped from St. Louis, for Fort Sam Houston could now store all it needed for any operation in Texas or Mexico. Warehouse construction began east of the Cavalry and Light Artillery Post.

By now the biggest threat to the nation's southern border was coming from the Mexican revolutionary Pancho Villa, whom it was feared would seek to draw the United States into direct conflict with the Mexican government by seizing El Paso.

On April 24, Brig. Gen. John J. Pershing was ordered from San Francisco to El Paso's Fort Bliss with his 3,500-member Eighth Brigade. Since Pancho Villa was seen by peasants of northern Mexico as a Robin Hood seeking to better their lot, and had met in Washington with President Wilson, in August 1914 Pershing invited Villa to join him in reviewing the troops at Fort Bliss. "He will yet do great

CAMP WILSON,
FORT SAM-HOUSTON TEXAS,

To house troops during the rapid buildup to defend the border with Mexico in 1916, Camp Wilson was set up on the site of Fort Sam Houston's 1911 Maneuver Camp east of North New Braunfels Avenue. The legendary Mexican revolutionary Francisco "Pancho" Villa, below, was the easily identifiable villain.

Gen. Francisco Villa
the cause of it all

things for his beloved Mexico," Pershing predicted after their meeting, in words that would return to haunt him.

In the next two years, however, Villa lost much of the power by which he could once count 40,000 revolutionaries at his command. Desperate to trigger an American move against the rival government in Mexico City, and to gain new supplies for his forces, Villa targeted not El Paso but the isolated settlement of Columbus, New Mexico, the temporary border post of the 13th Cavalry some 70 miles to the west.

During the night of March 8, 1916, Villa and 485 men slipped north across the border into Columbus. The raid began at 4 a.m. Villa's men shot up the town, executing six civilians at the local hotel and killing five others plus seven American soldiers. But they neither stampeded nor captured any of the cavalry's 200 horses, seized no munitions or money and quickly found themselves in the direct line of American machine gun fire.

As they retreated with the 13th Cavalry in pursuit, Villa's men left more than 100 of their own dead, nearly a fourth of their number.

Gen. Frederick Funston, commander of the Southern Department, headquartered at Fort Sam Houston, was summoned to Washington to confer with Secretary of War Newton Baker. They planned a two-pronged Punitive Expedition against Villa. U.S. troops would drive south from Columbus and from Hachita, 43 miles west. Villa would be surrounded at Boca Grande, the village 15 miles south of the border where he was reported to be holed up.

Command of the expeditionary force was a prize for any Army officer, and Funston wanted it badly. But Secretary of War Baker selected Pershing instead. That was "because I was on the ground," explained Pershing, who at Fort Bliss was 600 miles closer to Co-

lumbus than was General Funston in San Antonio. But Baker was concerned about reports that the highly popular Funston, who outranked Pershing and was five years younger, had a drinking problem. Funston would remain at Fort Sam Houston to supervise funneling of supplies to troops in northern Mexico.

When Pershing crossed the border a week after Villa's raid, he took soldiers of the 7th, 10th, 11th and 13th cavalries, the 6th and 16th infantries—his old 8th Brigade from San Francisco—and two batteries of the 6th Field Artillery. Also with him were Corps of Engineers, ambulance and wagon companies, a field hospital and Signal Corps detachments. The strike force numbered 4,800 men and 4,175 animals.

The First Aero Squadron, based at Fort Sam Houston's Aviation Post, had 15 pilots and 9 airplanes, Curtiss JN-3 "Jennies" and Burgesses. When news of the Columbus raid reached San Antonio, Benjamin Foulois, now a captain and squadron commander, began to prepare his men for combat duty, though he had yet to receive orders. Indeed, Secretary of War Baker directed Pershing "to make all practical use of the aeroplanes at San Antonio, Texas, for observation." On March 12 orders came to Foulois to proceed to Columbus.

Eight of the squadron's nine airplanes plus equipment were crated and loaded on a westbound train. With Foulois went 10 officers, 82 enlisted men and a civilian mechanic. In El Paso they picked up a medical doctor and three corpsmen.

After a 30-hour train ride, "we arrived at Columbus on March 15, 1916," wrote Foulois, "and immediately began unloading and assembling our planes. When the first one was ready the next day, Captain Townsend F. Dodd, my deputy, and I made the first reconnaissance flight 30 miles into Mexico—the first aerial reconnaissance by United States military aircraft ever made over foreign territory."

Foulois and Dodd saw nothing, meaning that the Mexicans were at least a day's march from Columbus. With this information, General Pershing ordered his forces southward.

On March 19, the planes took off for a flight toward Ascension, Mexico, 60 miles south of Columbus, on a two-day flight to Casas

With the pursuit of Pancho Villa inensifying, Gen. Frederick Funston, above center, commander of the U.S. Army's Fort Sam Houston-based Southern Department, met with Mexico's secretary of war, Gen. Alvaro Obregon, left above, in El Paso in the spring of 1916. Later in the year, at Fort Sam Houston, newly-arrived troops awaiting border assignments found diversion in football. Below, a crowd of soldiers watches the 1st Mississipi Infantry play the 3rd Wisconsin on the Infantry Post parade ground.

Eight of Fort Sam Houston's First Aero Squadron's nine planes were crated and sent by train to the Mexican border, where they were reassembled, above, as part of the expeditionary force commanded by Brig. Gen. John J. Pershing, below.

Grandes. Ten minutes into the flight, one plane dropped out of formation and returned to Columbus. Four planes actually arrived at Ascension, but it was already dark.

Lt. H. A. Dargue, pilot of the sixth plane, fell behind the main body, missed the bonfires marking the landing field and flew farther south, landing safely but lost in an open valley. Another, Lt. R. H. Willis, overshot the field by 40 miles and damaged his landing gear in open desert terrain. The eighth, Lt. E. S. Gorrell, landed 40 miles east of Ascension. The next morning, the four planes at Ascension flew on to Casas Grandes, only to discover neither American troops nor a safe landing area. Headquarters company was finally located at Colonia Dublan, a Mormon community 25 miles away.

Ordered to search for rebels near Lake Babicora, Foulois and Dodd made a grim discovery: the 90-horsepower Curtiss engine was no match for the Sierra Madres mountains. Returning to Colonia Dublan, Foulois saw Lt. Tom Bowen fly into a whirlwind and crash. Bowen survived, but his plane did not.

Since the government of then-president Venustiano Carranza refused Pershing the use of Mexican railroads, all supplies had to be carried either in newly acquired Dodge trucks—unpredictable in rough terrain—or by mules, even slower. Supplies of medicine and food were running low. Foulois was ordered to fly to Chihuahua City and seek help from American Consul Marion Letcher.

With the luck his squadron was having, Foulois felt a backup was needed and took Dodd, also with his own observer, in a second plane. One landed north of Chihuahua, the other south. Dodd found the American consul, who got the supplies, loaded them on a train and then took Dodd to see the governor of Chihuahua, who turned out to be an old schoolmate of Dodd's at the University of Illinois.

Foulois, however, was captured by peasants almost immediately after landing. He was marched into Chihuahua City to the tune of "Mata el Gringo!"—"Kill the Yankee!"—and imprisoned. Unfortunately, Dodd's old friend the governor had no jurisdiction over police matters and it was late in the day before Foulois was released.

On April 17, the squadron, reduced to three planes, lost a third when Dargue and Willis crashed during a photo reconnaissance mis-

Colors waving, some 122,000 American troops arrived at the Mexican border in 1916 to find Pancho Villa.

sion. Secretary Baker requested $500,000 from Congress for new planes. Twelve Curtiss R-2s were ordered, complete with machine-guns, cameras, bombs and radios. Foulois returned to Columbus to pick them up.

When they arrived, wrote Foulois, "We parked our remaining tired and battered Jennies on the side of the field and put a match to them. I didn't want to take any chances that somebody would order us to keep on flying them."

Unfortunately, the R-2s did little better than the Jennies.

By April 12, the American forces in general had come to a stand-still. Carranza's government, which was supposed to be supporting the U.S. Army's operation, was in fact opposing it. Pershing's expedition was 450 miles into the state of Chihuahua and nearing Durango, but it had yet to have a decisive encounter with Pancho Villa. The

The U.S. Army's field artillery seemed certain to do in the errant Mexican revolutionaries.

Members of the First Illinois Cavalry, just off the train at the Mexican border, found a world quite different from that at home.

line of supply from Fort Sam Houston was so long that, as General Funston, still smarting from having been passed over for command, was quick to point out, "troops in the rear guarding it consume nearly everything that can be brought up along it."

Two months later, Pershing learned that a large force of Carranza's federal soldiers was about 100 miles away, heading toward his headquarters camp. Pershing sent 10th Cavalry Capt. Charles T. Boyd and 76 soldiers to Colonia Dublan to check out the reports. Boyd's meeting with the Mexican commander ended in an argument about U.S. troops entering the town.

When the smoke cleared an hour later, 14 Americans were dead, including Boyd; another 30 to 40 were wounded and 25 were taken prisoner. The Mexicans suffered even greater casualties, including their commander, killed in the first volley.

War with Mexico seemed imminent. On June 18 Wilson mobilized the National Guard and sent 122,000 men to the border, freeing 30,000 regular Army soldiers to fight in Mexico. The first Guardsmen reached Fort Sam Houston on June 30. They stayed in tents in the hastily-formed Camp Wilson, on the site of the 1911 Maneuver Camp.

Adobe buildings form the backdrop for this temporary camp of U.S. troops newly arrived on the border.

Hoping for a confrontation with Pancho Villa, U.S. Army troops get into combat position.

Once camped in hillier areas of the Chihuahuan Desert, soldiers adopted the Mexican use of wattle fencing.

A Joint Mexican-American Commission trying to end the conflict began meeting in September in Connecticut, then moved to Atlantic City while Army engineers, battling searing heat and torrential rainstorms, completed a modern highway from Columbus to Colonia Dublan. New fleets of Dodge trucks began rolling in with supplies.

While negotiations dragged on, during the first week of January 1917 Villa was finally trapped in a battle at Torreon. Villa escaped, but was badly beaten. That was what Woodrow Wilson needed to get the American forces out of Mexico gracefully. The president declared victory and on January 12 sent Pershing the order to withdraw. By Februay 5, all 10,690 Americans, with their 9,307 horses and 2,500 refugees, were north of the border.

Sausage-shaped observation balloons like those briefly based at Fort Sam Houston had more lift and stability than spherical balloons, and were among the new military technologies tested during the Mexican border war.

Though Pancho Villa was never captured—he died when his car was ambushed in 1923—the border was essentially safe. Moreover, troops found the experience invaluable in fighting World War I, now only months away. The importance of motorized transport trucks was now understood, and a standardized model had been developed. "Rolling kitchens" reduced the need for commissary campsites. Shoe design was improved. The way was pointed to better aircraft design.

The buildup also pumped new life into San Antonio's economy and strengthened the military presence. And an unexpected change occurred in ethnic makeup.That the tens of thousands of Mexican refugees crowding into the city during the Mexican Revolution would transform the city ethnically and culturally was quickly understood. Not expected was establishment of a sizable Chinese community.

The tide of Chinese immigration to the United States began in the 1860s, as laborers were needed to build the Transcontinental Railroad. Though halted by the Chinese Exclusion Act of 1882, Chi-

Although Pancho Villa remained uncaptured, the maneuvers and testing of new weapons provided valuable training for the impending World War I. This early tank, a four-wheel drive truck with a 40-horsepower engine and six-man crew, was covered with a half inch of armor and carried two machine guns.

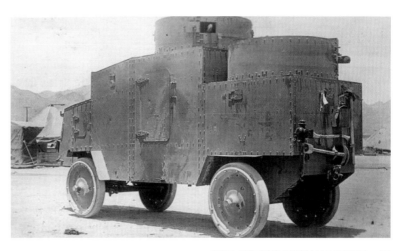

Lt. Dwight D. Eisenhower, a new West Point graduate, met his wife, Mamie, while first stationed at Fort Sam Houston, in 1916. The couple returned to live in an Infantry Post apartment after their marriage in Denver.

nese could still immigrate to Mexico. To reunite with newly arrived relatives, many left the United States to live in their own communities in Mexico, were they experienced severe discrimination. Pershing found them excellent scouts who provided valuable intelligence about Villa's movements. In retaliation, Villa let it be known that the Chinese would be slaughtered when Pershing left. Pershing succeeded in obtaining an immigration waiver so they could accompany him back into the United States.

Reaching Columbus with Pershing were 527 Chinese, all but 100 of them going on to San Antonio and arriving on June 7, 1917. They were boarded at the now nearly empty Camp Wilson, finding jobs as carpenters, blacksmiths, cooks and laborers until they could move into the civilian community, where many descendants remain.

One newly arrived soldier came not because of the border warfare but because of the flooding of an Army encampment to which he had been assigned on Galveston Island. Among the 19th Infantry troops pulled back to San Antonio was Lt. Dwight D. Eisenhower, newly graduated from West Point. Although sidelined from playing football by a knee injury, in San Antonio Eisenhower coached football at Peacock Military Academy and at St. Louis College, later St. Mary's University. He also met Mamie Doud, 18, whose family wintered in San Antonio. They were married at her home in Denver, Colorado, on July 1, 1916, the day Eisenhower was promoted to first lieutenant.

The next week the Eisenhowers returned to Fort Sam Houston to live in a two-room apartment on Infantry Post. He graduated from the post's new Bakers' and Cooks' School and did the cooking, while Mamie did the housework.

The separation so typical of Army life soon afflicted the Eisenhowers. As the prospect of war in Europe worsened, Lieutenant Eisenhower was moved to the Leon Springs Military Reservation. At Fort Sam Houston, Mamie, expecting their first child, became lonesome and telephoned that she was coming out to see him. No matter that he objected or that she couldn't drive.

As the angry lieutenant paced around the entrance, Mamie could be seen coming up Military Highway, her car weaving from side to side. Eisenhower was granted special permission to escort the mother-to-be back to the post.

7. Camp Travis and World War I

Members of Camp Travis's 18th Division form a human version of their symbol, the cactus, left. Field training was 26 miles away at Camp Funston, memorialized in a march before being renamed Camp Stanley, its mess hall tables below set for Thanksgiving Dinner in 1917.

Despite the neutrality of the United States after the outbreak of war in Europe in 1914, it was becoming clear that the country would be drawn into the war against Germany, especially with the rising number of American deaths on ships sunk by German submarines.

President Woodrow Wilson declared war on Germany on April 2, 1917, stating that "the world must be made safe for democracy."

For a commander of World War I's American Expeditionary Force, President Wilson turned to San Antonio. Gen. Frederick Funston had died unexpectedly in February and been replaced at Fort Sam Houston as commander of the Army's Southern Department by Gen. John J. Pershing, his Mexican border mission just completed.

Two months after moving into the commander's house on Staff Post Road, General Pershing bade farewell to San Antonians at a Battle of Flowers luncheon in the Menger Hotel and left for France.

But the nation was ill prepared to wage war overseas. As Pershing departed, only 5,000 volunteers had been recruited. A selective service system had yet to be implemented to bring military strength to 1.5 million. And that many soldiers needed new places to train. San Antonio would prove an excellent location, with its good weather and some sites already in place.

At the Leon Springs Military Reservation—renamed Camp Funston in memory of the late general—the First Officers Training Camp was established on May 8 to provide 90-day training for officer candidates. A processing station for cavalry horses was also established.

In this view looking east, Camp Travis sprawls beyond the end of the parade ground shared by the bordering Staff and Cavalry and Light Artillery posts and then ending at North New Braunfels Avenue. Above the open area at lower right is the Quadrangle, above it the Infantry Post parade ground and buildings.

Maj. Gen. H. T. Allen took his freshly-trained 90th Division from Camp Travis to France, opening space for the new 18th Division.

Soon, to avoid confusion with the Camp Funston already in Kansas, the Leon Springs facility was renamed Camp Stanley in honor of former Department of Texas commander Brig. Gen. David Stanley, and an additional 16,000 acres added nearby was designated Camp Bullis in memory of San Antonio's recently deceased Gen. John L. Bullis.

In early April 1917, the Aviation Section of the Army Signal Corps moved from Fort Sam Houston to a site picked by Capt. Benjamin Foulois southwest of San Antonio. First named Aviation Camp, the site was later redesignated Camp Kelly in memory of Lt. George E. M. Kelly, who had died when his plane crashed at Fort Sam Houston. The Army added four auxiliary fields near Camp Kelly, soon designated Kelly Field.

In another aviation development, members of the U.S. Army Balloon School arrived at Fort Sam Houston in January 1918. They stayed until barracks were completed three months later at Camp John Wise, west of Fort Sam Houston and north of San Antonio on the site of the present-day suburb of Olmos Park. The camp and its four observation balloons were moved to Brooks Field, near Kelly Field, at war's end.

Fort Sam Houston was well positioned for the new emergency by the warehouse construction and buildup to supply troops on the Mexican border. By the time war was declared, the Army was renting additional warehouse space throughout San Antonio and stockpiling and shipping ten times as many supplies as it had processed during the border war. As many as 64 railroad cars a week were arriving at post warehouses with supplies to be sorted and sent off to new Army camps throughout Texas, Oklahoma and New Mexico. Shortages, inevitably, occurred—in particular, in the winter of 1917–18, winter underwear and woolen stockings and, the next winter, woolen blankets.

Camp Travis (Avenue D, top) had a wireless station, left, and training areas, including for bayonets. Headquarters, above, marked Liberty Loan contributions. Right, the Co. MG, 358th Infantry, kitchen crew. Bottom, "the world's largest laundry."

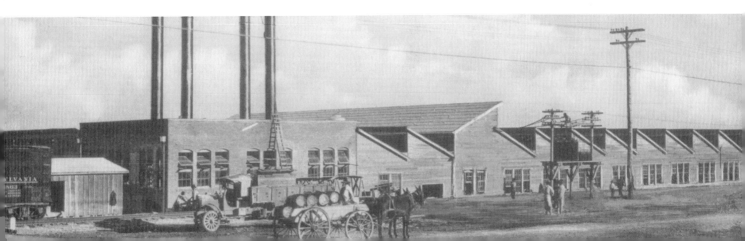

The Camp Travis theater was built by the Interstate Amusement Company and could seat 1,963 persons. It opened with a vaudeville show on January 6, 1918, and also showed silent films. Six months later it was purchased by the War Department and its name was changed from the Majestic Camp Theatre to Liberty Theatre. The theater organ was later moved to the post's Gift Chapel.

The post's most visible expansion in the war effort, however, would occur in its training facilities. As elsewhere in the nation, in Texas the Army was throwing up sprawling new camps to train entire divisions—Camp Bowie at Fort Worth and Camp MacArthur at Waco, both with lifetimes not outlasting the war. Fort Sam Houston already had Camp Wilson, easily expandable for training a division.

Raw recruits pouring into Camp Travis, right, had to be turned into disciplined fighting men in a minimum of time. Much of the job went to the notorious "Top Sergeant," below, characterized from experience by Pvt. S. L. Brannon.

An adjoining 1,280 acres was purchased to the northeast and the site was renamed Camp Travis, in memory of Alamo defender William Barret Travis.

On July 6, 1917, construction began over 800 acres, from North New Braunfels Avenue north and east to the future site of Brooke General Hospital. The project employed 3,700 carpenters and 4,500 plumbers, electricians, teamsters and general laborers. Using 35 million board feet of lumber, 60,000 doors and windows, and 210 miles of electrical wire, they built a city of 1,268 wooden buildings that could accommodate 46,000 soldiers and 13,000 animals.

Camp Travis buildings were connected by 25 miles of roads and 12 miles of railroad tracks, and were serviced by 61 miles of water and sewer pipes. The Fuel and Forage Office's yards at one point held 16,000 tons of coal and 3,000 cords of wood to heat the camp. The Camp Travis Laundry, with 425 civilian employees—300 of them the wives of soldiers—served units as far away as Kelly Field and washed two million pieces of clothes a month. The adjoining dry cleaning plant handled 70,000 pieces monthly.

Two months after construction began, Camp Travis began welcoming its first recruits, primarily from Texas and Oklahoma. Several thousand Oklahoma recruits were Indians, many of them chiefs made millionaires by recent oil discoveries but who had to adapt to the ways of other soldiers, who were making $30 a month. The new arrivals formed the 90th Division, under the command of Maj. Gen. Henry T. Allen. The division's junior officer candidates, most from the same region, were trained at the officer school at Camp Funston/Stanley.

In June 1918, General Allen, though at 58 one of the Army's oldest commanders, led the 31,000-member 90th Division to France. Its performance caused General Pershing to rate it one of the Army's top six overseas divisions.

After the 90th Division left, Camp Travis became an induction and training center for some 34,000 troops. They coalesced in late summer into the 18th Division, which took as its symbol the cactus and became known as the Cactus Division.

Like any city of its size, Camp Travis developed its own recreational and social infrastructure. There were recreation buildings sponsored by the YMCA and the Knights of Columbus, a library sponsored by the American Library Association, a Convalescent House

With many recruits having college football experience, Camp Travis players, scrimmaging at right, got their own football stadium. Its Thanksgiving Day dedication in 1917 was marred by a 12-7 loss to Kelly Field.

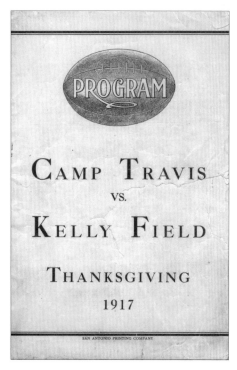

PROGRAM

CAMP TRAVIS

VS.

KELLY FIELD

THANKSGIVING

1917

SAN ANTONIO PRINTING COMPANY

run by the American Red Cross and the Interstate Amusement Company's theater, its capacity nearly 2,000.

Athletics in off hours included divisional field meets, baseball games and swimming meets. Football, however, drew the biggest crowds. In 1917, Camp Travis's $10,000 frame Military Athletic Stadium was completed just in time to be dedicated at the Thanksgiving Day game between red-and-white Camp Travis and green-and-white Kelly Field.

The diversity of recent college football backgrounds among players on both teams was reflected by that of their coaches: Kelly Field coaches included former stars from West Point and Virginia Military Institute and onetime captains of Harvard and Princeton teams, while the lone "mainstay" of the Camp Travis staff had starred at the University of Wisconsin.

Kelly Field's abundance of coaching talent may have influenced the outcome; some 20,000 soldiers watched Kelly Field defeat the home team 12-7.

On Thanksgiving Day 1918, Camp Travis lost again to Kelly Field, this time by a score of 20-3, "after several of the best Camp Travis players had been carried off the field injured." That year Camp Travis gridders did manage a 12-7 victory over Texas A&M College and tied a no-score game with Waco's Camp MacArthur.

Near the end of the war, a medical crisis sweeping the nation hit Camp Travis, far more serious than the customary venereal disease that inflicted many soldiers; the General Wartime Commission of Churches had declared that even though the unofficially sanctioned brothel district west of San Pedro Creek downtown supposedly was closed, that neighborhood was still far too popular with soldiers, and San Antonio "presented one of the most serious moral situations in the country."

On September 30, 1918, the nationwide epidemic of Spanish influenza—that caused 87,000 Americans to die in one 10-week period alone—struck Camp Travis. On that day, 51 cases were reported at the camp hospital. The next day, 268 more were reported. On the

This mobile recruiting effort could have been an entry in a San Antonio parade.

third day, the entire camp was quarantined, and all of San Antonio was declared off limits.

The peak number of new cases was reported by the camp surgeon, Maj. A. L. Van Meter, on October 7, eight days after the outbreak began: 1,073. The day also began the hospital's daily count of the dead. For a full month at least one soldier died each day. New patients were quarantined from the rest of the camp in wards of tents.

For six weeks Camp Travis itself remained quarantined. An average of 158 nurses served 58 wards in two major buildings and four nearby barracks buildings, plus tents. Finally, at 4:30 p.m. on November 11, 1918, the day the armistice was signed in France, the quarantine was lifted.

Even the dimished fear of contagion could not deter jubilant troops from rejoicing. With the quarantine removed, reported the *San Antonio Daily Express*, "soldiers streamed out of the big cantonment as fast as cars could carry them, many making the long trip to the city on foot when the supply of cars became exhausted."

Major Van Meter's final tally listed 11,372 cases. There were 1,927 civilian deaths in San Antonio and 201 at Camp Travis, a percentage considered low in comparison with other Army camps.

The Camp Travis Hospital's 150-plus nurses played a vital role during the devastating influenza epidemic of 1918, which caused 201 deaths at the camp.

At the end of World War I, the Camp Travis-trained 90th Division returned to a hero's welcome at the Alamo, complete with a triumphal arch inscribed with names of the division's campaigns.

With the war over, the 90th Division was welcomed back to San Antonio with a parade culminating in a march through a wooden triumphal arch modeled after the one on the Champs Elysee in Paris and built in front of the Alamo.

Most members of the 18th Division, their training unfinished, were discharged and went home. Camp Travis, which had trained some 112,000 troops during the war, became a demobilization center. By the time the center closed in March 1919, it had processed and discharged some 62,500 soldiers arriving from wartime posts.

While the hastily built divisional camps elsewhere were being shut down and their land sold, Camp Travis, administratively absorbed by Fort Sam Houston in 1922, was kept open to house the Second Division.

8. The Houston Riot Courts-Martial

At 8:50 on the night of August 23, 1917, hell came to Houston. One of the nation's most notorious race riots, near the Army's Camp Logan, resulted in 20 deaths.

The ensuing trials at Fort Sam Houston of 118 black soldiers became the largest courts-martial in the history of the U.S. Army. They also resulted in one major reform of the military justice system.

The strict racial segregation common in the South since the end of the Civil War frequently led to conflict between civilians and black soldiers, who were still subject to discrimination within the Army but frequently from areas less restrictive than the Deep South, as Robert Haynes notes in *A Night of Violence: The Houston Riot of 1917* (Louisiana State University Press, 1976).

In late July 1917, men of the all-black 3rd Battalion, 24th Infantry left Camp Furlong at Columbus, New Mexico, for Houston, where they were to guard the construction of Camp Logan. They expected a choice assignment, since Houston was a large, modern city with a sizable black population.

Men of the all-black 3rd Battalion, 24th Infantry expected Houston to be a choice assignment.

During their first outing in town, however, the black soldiers were ignored in shops and forced to ride trolleys with signs directing them to the rear. Though accustomed to segregation, many had not been subjected to such scorn. On at least two occasions, infuriated soldiers ripped down the signs or moved into the "whites only" area due to overcrowding in the rear. One soldier threatened to commandeer the car and throw the conductor off if the signs were put up again.

Pvt. Alonzo Edwards watched the arrest of a black woman charged with harboring a young black boy suspected of having been involved in an illegal craps game. Edwards loudly offered to pay any fine if she was released, but he was struck with a pistol and taken to the police station. Camp Logan's provost officer of the day, Cpl. Charles Baltimore, also a black, went to the police station to learn the details, only to be hit on the head, chased and arrested.

When the story got back to the camp, Baltimore, by then released, was said to have been shot and killed by the policemen. When a white mob was reported—falsely—to be moving on the camp, black soldiers began loading rifles and fixing bayonets. For 15 minutes they fired indiscriminately. Sgt. Vida Henry led more than 100 armed black soldiers in formation toward the center of town.

But the men quickly broke ranks, and bands of six or seven began roaming the streets. As one car approached a restaurant it was

At "the largest murder trial in the history of the United States," held in Fort Sam Houston's Gift Chapel, the accused sat in rows at the left and the panel of judges sat in the altar area.

fired upon. The driver died instantly. Two men leaving a streetcar were ambushed. One died. Rufus Daniels, the policeman involved in Corporal Baltimore's "death," left his car to charge soldiers lying prone in the roadway, only to die in a hail of bullets, his body then battered with rifle butts and bayonetted.

An Army captain in an approaching car tried to calm one group but was mistaken for a policeman; he died in another hail of bullets with the other passengers, three enlisted men and a police officer.

When the rioters realized they had killed an Army officer, they became more subdued. Just after 2 a.m., as Sgt. William Nesbit successfully got the last of the rioters headed back to Camp Logan, Sergeant Henry, who had initially tried to control the men, shot himself.

The worst of the riot had lasted just two hours. When it ended the toll was 19 dead, including 15 whites—4 of them police officers—and 4 black soldiers. Twelve were seriously wounded, one of whom—a policeman—soon died. It was the nation's first race riot in which more whites than blacks died.

In the morning, Houston authorities imposed a curfew on the city. The next day, the Army slipped the Third Battalion onto a waiting train back to New Mexico, where, in a plea bargain, seven riot participants agreed to testify against the others.

Fort Sam Houston had jurisdiction for general courts-martial and was chosen as the site. They began on November 1, 1917, and lasted for nearly five months, until March 26, 1918.

The Gift Chapel was chosen as the site of the first trial. The 118 accused sat in rows of wooden slat chairs on a platform facing the altar, to improve their view of the witness stand. Sgt. William Nesbit, the highest-ranking accused, sat in the front row chair closest to the altar area. There sat the panel of judges: three brigadier generals, seven colonels and three lieutenant colonels. Brig. Gen. George K. Hunter, who had the highest seniority, was named president of the court. The pews were packed with witnesses and spectators.

To find the defendants guilty, the panel of 13 needed a simple majority of seven. For sentencing, military law required two-thirds, or nine votes. Since World War I was under way, the soldiers were charged with violating four of the Articles of War during wartime: the 64th, willfully disobeying a superior officer; the 66th, mutiny— breaking out of camp and attacking the City of Houston; the 92nd, willful and premeditated murder; and the 93rd, assaulting a civilian.

The role of defense counsel for the 63 accused in the first trial went to Maj. Harry S. Grier, ranking defense attorney in the Southern Department, who had arrived at his new assignment less than two weeks earlier. Assuming that all white officers were on the same side, defendants refused to speak with him. Prosecutors planned to base much of their case on the testimony of Capt. Bartlett James, officer of the day when the riot began, but on October 25 he was found dead of a self-inflicted gunshot wound.

The verdict in the first trial was announced December 9, 11 days after the final testimony. Of the 63 defendants, 5 were acquitted. The others were convicted on charges ranging from assault to mutiny to disobedience and, for 13 soldiers, to murder. Those 13 were sentenced to death, the others to sentences from two years to life.

The next evening, those sentenced to death were transferred from the cavalry guardhouse—later the post library, now part of the Education Center—to a barracks building. Before sunrise they were awakened for their final trip. To avoid press coverage, rumors that the execution would be at Camp Stanley were leaked to newsmen.

As reporters raced to Camp Stanley, at about 6:20 a.m. the soldiers left the barracks in the company of Bexar County Sheriff John Tobin, a doctor, 7 deputies, 125 cavalrymen, 100 infantrymen, 2 white Army chaplains and a black civilian minister. The procession stopped at a grove of mesquites along Salado Creek at the eastern edge of Camp Travis, where the Corps of Engineers, by the light of bonfires, had built a large wooden scaffold.

In the moments before the trapdoors in the gallows floor swung down, almost no one spoke. Only a "good-bye to the Boys of Company C" was heard. Once the doctor pronounced each man dead, he was lowered to the ground and placed in one of 13 graves dug nearby. The engineers who had so quickly built the gallows dismantled the structure and burned it on the site.

The second court-martial was held in the Infantry Post gymnasium. Fifteen soldiers were accused of leaving their posts and of the premeditated murder of E. M. Jones.

As reporters raced to Camp Stanley, those sentenced to die were taken to a gallows near Salado Creek.

Pvt. Ezekial Bullock agreed to serve as witness for the prosecution in exchange for immunity for himself. On the stand, he named the five accused who, with him, had fired several rounds into an approaching car, killing its driver, E. M. Jones.

The jury panel, almost identical to the one in the earlier case, deliberated for less than three hours. Results were the same: the five accused of murder were found guilty and sentenced to death by hanging. The others were found guilty only of abandoning their posts. Each was sentenced to prison at hard labor. This time, before the executions were carried out, the case was reviewed by President Wilson and Secretary of War Baker.

While these final decisions were pending, the third court-martial got under way. This one was based on new evidence linking another 11 soldiers with the riot. Their fates followed those of the others, at least through the sentencing stage.

By now the nation was weary with news of the trials. Backlash in white communities had led to further racial polarization and the injury and death of innocent blacks. After conversations with several black leaders, President Wilson commuted 10 of the 11 death sentences to life in prison. He concurred on the 6 remaining death sentences—the 5 from the second trial and 1 from the last court-martial—"because the persons involved were found guilty by plain evidence of having deliberately, under circumstances of shocking brutality, murdered designated and peaceably disposed civilians."

But when the official orders arrived at Fort Sam Houston, something was unclear. Consequently, as the sun rose above the Salado Creek on September 16, 1918, the five defendants in the second case died on the gallows. When the War Department received this word, it immediately contacted Fort Sam Houston's judge advocate general, Col. A. S. Ansel. Why had the sole defendant sentenced to die in the third trial been spared? The reason: No orders were ever received naming Private Boone. Still another week passed before those orders arrived. Boone was hanged on the morning of September 24.

Others found guilty in the second and third courts-martial received sentences of varying length in federal prison.

Of all 118 soldiers finally charged with participation in the Houston riot, 110 were found guilty of at least one crime. One was relieved of his sentence due to poor health, 19 died on the gallows and the rest did federal prison time, including 53 originally assigned life sentences. Most of those imprisoned were paroled by the end of the 1920s through efforts of the National Association for the Advancement of Colored People.

Not carried out were the recommendations of the inspector general of the Army, Brig. Gen. John I. Chamberlain, and the inspector general of the Southern Department, Col. G. C. Cress, that three white officers—a captain, a major and a colonel—be court-martialed for bungling an extremely volatile situation.

There was a positive outcome of the trials. The national outcry following the secret executions resulted in a major change in mili-

One result of the courts-martial was a major change in the military justice system.

After the hangings on hastily-built gallows near Salado Creek at the eastern edge of Camp Travis, bodies were lowered into numbered graves and the gallows structure was burned.

tary trial procedure: thereafter, any case within the United States that produced a sentence of death must be examined and approved by both the president and the secretary of war—now the secretary of defense—before being carried out.

The 24th Infantry continued as an all-black regiment until October 1, 1951, when the Army implemented President Harry Truman's order to end segregation in the armed forces of the United States.

Within a few years of the extension of Fort Sam Houston's parade grounds eastward through the
site of Camp Travis, and construction of Spanish Colonial Revival officers' quarters along
the northern edge, traditional reviews of field artillery units changed from mounted
cavalry and horse-drawn caissons to a fully mechanized force.

9. A Time of Transition

Soldiers who stayed in the scaled-back Army after World War I found themselves dealing with a changed military world. The next two decades would find them adapting to the new mechanized warfare featuring tanks, trucks and aircraft rather than the animals that for millennia had carried soldiers and hauled artillery and supplies.

Fort Sam Houston would also undergo major organizational and physical changes. The National Defense Act of 1920 reorganized the Army into nine corps areas, the largest being that of the Eighth Corps, headquartered at Fort Sam Houston under the command of Maj. Gen. Joseph Dickman. The Eighth Corps comprised Army installations in Texas, Arizona, New Mexico, Oklahoma, Colorado and part of Wyoming. Fort Sam Houston would serve as a garrison for the Second Division.

During the interlude soldiers also dealt with a more benign technical innovation of recent years—movies, as a growing film industry often looked to the unique assets of San Antonio. In 1925, Fort Sam Houston provided trucks and soldiers as extras for a major scene in director King Vidor's classic *The Big Parade*. The next year, several thousand Second Division soldiers were filmed for key scenes in two movies: *Wings*, directed by William Wellman and starring Clara Bow and Buddy Rogers, and winner of the first Academy Award for Best Picture, and *The Rough Riders*, directed by Victor Fleming, its stars including Noah Beery and Mary Astor.

In 1925, thousands of Fort Sam Houston soldiers went to Camp Stanley as extras in two movies—the Academy Award-winning *Wings*, including the filmed portrayal below of the Battle of St. Mihiel, and *The Rough Riders*.

In 1925, 23rd Infantry soldiers, with occasional 10-minute stops to rest and water horses, headed to Fredericksburg on a typical field exercise, accompanied by horse-drawn supply trains—that also drew field kitchens, bottom left—and a motorcycle-escorted headquarters unit, to the campsite, lower right.

Dodd Field was named in 1928 for pioneer Fort Sam Houston aviator Col. Townsend Dodd. This view looks north beyond Winans Road. Angling from lower left toward upper right is Harry Wurzbach Highway, to its west the undeveloped land that would become part of the suburb of Terrell Hills.

At Camp Stanley, soldiers reenacted the World War I Battle of St. Mihiel for *Wings* on the same day other soldiers nearby at Camp Bullis were restaging the charge up San Juan Hill for *The Rough Riders*. For *Wings*, fliers and personnel also came in from four posts elsewhere. Fort Sam Houston contributed the use of $16 million in government equipment, including tanks, artillery and explosives.

In gratitude, when the world premier of *Wings* was held at San Antonio's Texas Theater on Houston Street in 1926, the nearly $5,500 in opening night proceeds was donated for the Second Division War Monument under construction in Washington, D.C.

One of Fort Sam Houston's early aviators was remembered in 1928 with the naming of the airfield at the northern end of the post in honor of Col. Townsend F. Dodd, who was killed in an air crash in 1919. The area remains known as Dodd Field, even though the airfield, opened in 1915, closed before the start of World War II.

Soldiers did not have to worry about where their next paycheck was coming from after the Great Depression began spreading through the nation in 1929, but they did help others combat the effects. In mid-1933 Camp Bullis was used to process some 4,000 civilians who signed up for the government-financed Civilian Conservation Corps to work on public construction and conservation projects, many of those in the San Antonio area.

Early in 1934, Fort Sam Houston became home to 300 members of a unit providing administrative and logistic support to all 10,000 members of the Texas District of the Civilian Conservation Corps, who were housed in barracks on the site of the present-day Post Exchange.

At this time Fort Sam Houston was winding up a construction project that transformed the site of Camp Travis, its buildings de-

Removal of Camp Travis (page 58) cleared the way for Spanish Colonial Revival style construction in 1929–39 of New Post on either side of the parade ground extension past North New Braunfels Avenue, horizontally bisecting view above.

New Post's Commander's House is at left, quarters for non-commissioned officers below left, officers, below, and enlisted men, bottom.

Brooke Army Medical Center was built at the end of the parade ground, off top picture at left.

Support facilities in the same style, included, on the facing page, the post exchange at top and, below left center, the gas station and post theater.

Post exchange complex interiors on the facing page show the main shopping area, one room of the restaurant and the "grocery department," predecessor of the commissary.

Military horsemanship skills carried over into recreation, as shown by these three members of the 12th Field Artillery's 1937 polo team.

signed to last only seven years. Indeed, not long after the end of the war the Camp Travis complex was deteriorating badly, roofs leaking and stairways collapsing. Similar military housing conditions elsewhere led to the Army Housing Program of 1926. New construction was to follow the latest concepts of civilian city planning, the War Department directed, adapting regional architectural themes to buildings served by adequate streets and utilities, essentially comprising a self-contained city.

The War Department hired George B. Ford as its national city planning advisor. For its design at Fort Sam Houston, the Army hired San Antonio architect Atlee B. Ayres, noted for his local work in the newly popular regional Spanish Colonial Revival architecture already being used for construction projects at California's San Diego Naval Air Station and at El Paso's Fort Bliss. Ayres would also soon design the landmark headquarters building at San Antonio's new Randolph Field.

By mid-1927, Camp Travis's decaying buildings had been emptied by the temporary reassignment of the Second Division's Engineer Regiment to Fort Logan, Colorado, and its brigade to Fort Warren, Wyoming. By the following year nearly all 1,200 frame buildings had been cleared from Camp Travis's 800-acre site. Without the wartime emergency that triggered the hasty construction of Camp Travis, architects and planners designed New Post on the Camp Travis site. The $6 million project would take just over 10 years.

The original parade ground's eastern end along North New Braunfels Avenue had intentionally been left unenclosed by earlier planners, who believed it might someday be extended across the street to the east. Now it was, first directly east and then northeast in an identical width. It was eventually named Arthur MacArthur Field in honor of the father of Gen. Douglas MacArthur, once stationed at the post.

As officers' quarters lined the northern edge of the old parade ground, so were New Post's 157 standardized Spanish Colonial Revival housing units platted along the northern edge of Arthur MacArthur Field, which was also faced by a new Officers' Club. Likewise, 140 smaller family quarters for noncommissioned officers were built south of the new parade ground, in addition to nine three-story barracks buildings for enlisted men.

Among other new buildings south of Arthur MacArthur Field were a movie theater with an ornamental mission-style tower, noncommissioned officers' club, post exchange, commissary, football stadium, baseball grandstand, radio station and communications building, prison and, for the cavalry and artillery, 29 new stables, sheds and shops. A Consolidated Motor Pool symbolized the shift from horse-drawn to motorized vehicles.

At the northern end of what had become Arthur MacArthur Field, on the site of the Camp Travis hospital, went the new eight-story, 418-bed hospital. The area had been named Argonne Heights in honor of the Second Division's participation in the Argonne Forest campaign in France during World War I. On opening day, February 7,

Brooke Army Medical Center opened in 1938 at the head of the newly-extended parade ground on Argonne Heights, site of the Camp Travis hospital complex. On either side of the main building were quarters for nurses, left, and enlisted men, right. The eight- story main building had an initial capacity of 418 beds.

1938, 12 ambulances shuttled 324 patients from the old Station Hospital. By noon, the hospital already had done its first emergency operation, an appendectomy.

Already obvious to the medical officer in charge, Col. Lee Hart, that even this facility would soon be overcrowded, the War Department immediately allocated $450,000 for a 200-bed wing. In 1942 it was named in honor of Brig. Gen. Roger Brooke, who had died two years earlier while commanding the Medical Field Service School at Carlisle Barracks, Pennsylvania.

During an assignment at Fort Sam Houston that began in 1928, Brooke, a specialist in tuberculosis and other infectious diseases, played an important role in uniting the region's military and civilian medical groups.

West of the hospital, quarters were completed in 1937 for 50 nurses, a building named Reid Hall in honor of Capt. Elizabeth D. Reid, chief nurse at Fort Sam Houston during World War I and later chief of the Army Nursing Corps. To the east went a barracks for the 220-man medical detachment.

When the project was completed, George B. Ford, the War Department's planning advisor, pointed to Fort Sam Houston as one

In an Army dependent on reliable animals for mobility, horses and mules were treated with respect even after their useful service had ended. At top left, Verdun, an artillery mule in World War I, was led in a San Antonio Fiesta parade in 1928.

Fort Sam Houston's best-known horse was Pat, top right, brought into cavalry service in 1912 but, after being retired, retained as a symbol until his death in 1953, at the age of 45. Pat was buried beneath a headstone on Staff Post. With Pat at left is then-Maj. Maxwell Taylor, later chairman of the Joint Chiefs of Staff.

One of thousands of unsung horses was Dick, shown above at G Company's Cavalry Post stables in the World War I era with Lt. Charlie Janworth.

of the few Army posts where "sheer beauty of layout" had been achieved.

While construction of New Post thrust Fort Sam Houston into a new era, the past was still represented by the little-changed historic areas of the post and the transition era of the present by living artifacts. One was a celebrity of sorts—"Arizona Bill," a former Indian scout whose weathered face, steel wool hair, chin whiskers, slouch hat and leather breeches made him a familiar sight on post.

Born Raymond Hatfield Gardner, Arizona Bill had been kidnapped by Comanches when he was one. At nine, he was traded to a Sioux tribe for nine ponies, nine blankets and two girls. As a young boy he served as a scout for Union forces during the Civil War, then drifted through the West until, on January 28, 1887, he enlisted in the Army at Fort Reno, Indian Territory, signing his enlistment papers with a bold "X."

Eighth Corps Commander Maj. Gen. Johnson Hagood permitted the homeless veteran to live out his life at any Army installation within his jurisdiction. With his white mule, Tipperary, Arizona Bill came to Fort Sam Houston. Preferring the company of Tipperary to most people, he lived alongside his mule in stables near Artillery Post.

Arizona Bill died in 1940 on the fifty-third anniversary of his Army enlistment. He was buried in a civilian cemetery, the military records which would have qualified him to be buried in a military cemetery having been lost. M.Sgt. George Miller, however, determined to find them. In November 1976, Miller's long search was at last successful, and Arizona Bill was reinterred with full honors in Fort Sam Houston's National Cemetery.

Another living relic was Pat, a cavalry horse brought into the Army in 1912. In 1938, when the 12th Field Artillery's stables were converted into garages for motorized vehicles, at the request of the soldiers Pat was permitted to be retained in "retired" status. He lived near an old Artillery Post paddock until his death in 1953 at the advanced age of 45. He was buried in a Staff Post field beneath a distinctive headstone, funded by the Second Division Association.

One living reminder that effective change is not always accomplished quickly came in the person of Brig. Gen. Billy Mitchell, the

"Arizona Bill," an Indian Wars veteran who ended his years, as he wished, living in a Fort Sam Houston stable with his trusty mule, Tipperary, was a well-known figure on post. They are shown in 1939 during a Fiesta visit of King Antonio XXI (J. Layton Cochran) with, continuing from left, then-Maj. Gen. H. J. Brees and then-Maj. Gen. Walter Krueger.

wartime Assistant Chief of Air Service and a strident opponent of the reduction of the Army's military aviation program. In 1921, Mitchell staged two air raids off the Virginia coast that sank several derelict ships in a controversial effort to dramatize the value of military airpower. Ever critical of the military's aviation policies, Mitchell was finally reduced to the rank of colonel and transferred to Fort Sam Houston in early 1925 in hopes that he would be silent.

Yet a few months later, Mitchell delivered to the press a withering assessment of the military's handling of a series of aircraft disasters. Mitchell was sent from San Antonio to Washington, where he was court-martialed and convicted of insubordination, though his stands ultimately proved correct.

As Fort Sam Houston's Maneuver Camp of 1911 provided training in new military techniques that would prove useful during World War I, so did a major exercise at Fort Sam Houston in 1937 consolidate the changes in technology brought with World War I and preview strategies that would become pivotal in World War II.

The 1937 exercise, under Maj. Gen. Herbert J. Brees, was the largest military maneuver since the end of World War I. Refined in further field exercises during the next two years at Camp Bullis, it led to development of a military strategy called the Triangular Division, which became the basic structure of the modern mechanized Army.

The traditional division comprised 21,060 enlisted men and 987 officers, 6,800 horses and mules and 750 automobiles and supply trucks, all divided into four regiments of infantry supported by three regiments of artillery and an ammunition train.

The new Triangular Division reduced the traditional division's four infantry regiments to three—with 12,800 enlisted men and 690 officers—and reduced the three artillery regiments to one, all sup-

Seen in review looking south from atop Brooke General Hospital is the fully mechanized Second Division, Fort Sam Houston's major tenant between World Wars I and II.

ported by 1,600 automobiles and trucks, but no animals. A cavalry reconnaissance squadron preceded the main body of troops, in scout cars and motorcycles rather than on horseback. Instead of sabers and carbines, its troops used .50 caliber machine guns.

The result was not the cumbersome organizational structure that had frustrated General Pershing in his pursuit of the fast-moving Pancho Villa through northern Mexico, but a fast-moving strike force. It was a structure that would be used successfully in combat during the upcoming World War II and the Korean War.

10. World War II

Fort Sam Houston, barely settled in its newly expanded facilities, faced an abrupt change after the Nazi invasion of France in May 1940, which caused President Franklin Roosevelt to mobilize the National Guard and begin expanding the military to meet the perceived threat to the United States. Almost immediately, a Recruit Reception Center opened in a tent city at Fort Sam Houston's Dodd Field to process as many as 1,000 recruits each week.

Replacement of the quickly thrown up Camp Travis had hardly been completed when, once again, a Camp Travis–like mini-city of temporary barracks burst onto the post. From 1940 to 1941, more than 400 standardized frame buildings were hastily completed, with another 100 added during the next four years.

Annual maneuvers took on a new sense of urgency. In 1941 the Third Army successfully "defended" the maneuver area in northern Louisiana from the Second Army, "invading" from southern Arkansas. Involved in planning was Fort Sam Houston's Third Army Com-

Happy members of the 36th Division, Texas National Guard, mobilized at Dodd Field, depart for Christmas leave in 1940.

World War II brought inspections of the 2nd Tank Co., top left, and, top right, of the 38th Field Artillery. There were flyovers during reviews, test drives of the new "reconnaissance cars"—jeeps—and formal flag raisings on the parade ground.

Marches and caravans to Camp Bullis for field training, below left, also accelerated. Below right, vehicles of the 28th Medical Detachment pass the Camp Bullis mess halls.

Marching at Dodd Field, above, are members of Texas A&M University's junior and senior classes who enlisted as a body in 1943.

mander Lt. Gen. Walter Kreuger's new chief of staff, Col. Dwight D. Eisenhower.

When Eisenhower and his wife, Mamie, returned to San Antonio for their second tour of duty—on July 1, 1941, their 25th wedding anniversary—they arrived as they had from their honeymoon a quarter century before, aboard a train. This time, instead of driving to Fort Sam Houston over rough streets to a two-room officers' quarters flat, they were chauffeured in a staff car to the two-story brick 179 Artillery Post Road, with its sweeping verandas and unencumbered view of the parade ground across the way. In September, Eisenhower's promotion to brigadier general came through. His wife pinned on the stars in a ceremony on the parade ground.

After their Sunday lunch at home on December 7, 1941, Eisenhower was napping before returning to the office—staff officers were working weekends as tension mounted in the Pacific—when Mamie heard on the radio about the Japanese attack on Peral Harbor. She woke him just before the phone rang, summoning him to his office.

During World War II, 27,000-acre Camp Bullis served primarily as an infantry training ground, but also hosted a reception and training center for draftees and a prisoner of war camp. Its main cluster of facilities is shown below.

A variety of shops like the one at right kept Fort Sam Houston running during World War II, also maintaining such weaponry as the machine guns, below, lined up beside barracks along the parade grounds.

In the coming years, four of World War II's great military leaders left Fort Sam Houston for wartime assignments.

One week after Pearl Harbor General Eisenhower left for Washington, having been picked by Gen. George Marshall as assistant chief of staff for the Operations Division. Six months later he was sent to North Africa on a path to becoming supreme commander of Allied forces in Europe and, eventually, president of the United States.

General Krueger stayed in San Antonio to oversee training the Third Army for combat in Europe, then in early 1943 was sent on his own to Australia to command the new Sixth Army's campaign through the South Pacific. It fell to Maj. Gen. Courtney Hodges to lead the Third Army from Fort Sam Houston to Europe and to reassignments that led to command of the First Army.

To fill the void left when Third Army troop trains pulled out of San Antonio, in January 1944 Lt. Gen. William Simpson brought the Fourth Army from California. Using some of its personnel, he organized the Ninth Army. While the Fourth Army remained at Fort Sam Houston, General Simpson took the Ninth Army to England. With the First Army of General Hodges and the Third Army of Gen. George Patton, it formed the nucleus of the American forces that reached Berlin in April 1945 and ended the war in Europe.

These changes at the highest level reflected the frenetic activity elsewhere. More than 240 units were based at Fort Sam Houston at some point during the war, 150 of them ending up overseas. Eighty

Members of the 30th Women's Auxiliary Corps Post Headquarters Company stand in formation after arriving in San Antonio by train in December 1942.

World War II era cooks and KP workers lined up for a photo in this barracks mess hall.

percent of those went to the European Theater and the rest to the Pacific. As many as one million soldiers passed through the post.

Headquarters of five of the nine field armies overseas—the Third, Sixth, Ninth, Tenth and Fifteenth—were trained at Fort Sam Houston, as were three infantry divisions and several smaller units. Units from Fort Sam Houston participated in 28 of the 36 campaigns against Axis forces throughout the world. During the last 12 months of the war, the Fourth Army, its headquarters in Fort Sam Houston's quadrangle, shipped 16 divisions with some 350,000 men overseas.

The Provost Marshal General School was set up to train military police and officer candidates, and the Adjutant General School moved to the post. Near the Southern Pacific Railroad yards to the south, Camp Cushing was set up to train railway operations battalions. It was named in honor of Col. Edward B. Cushing, a noted military and civilian railroad civil engineer. The San Antonio Army Service Forces Depot was expanded, and employed more than 2,500 civilians.

Brooke General Hospital's patient capacity soared to 10,000 as the medical detachment's barracks and many New Post barracks were converted to wards for convalescents, those awaiting transfer to other hospitals and wounded soldiers. Three barracks buildings linked as an addition in 1944 were later named the Beach Pavilion to honor a onetime Fort Sam Houston Station Hospital commander, Maj. Gen. George C. Beach Jr. The renovated old Station Hospital on Artillery Post handled infectious and contagious diseases and neuropsychiatric patients, those moved to a new building in mid-1942.

As the war unfolded, the Army Adjutant General's office determined that 406 of 628 military occupations could be handled by women, who if trained could free 3.9 million men for combat duty within a year. Overcoming their reservations, the Army began recruiting volunteers for the new Women's Auxiliary Army Corps. When

As women entered the Army for the first time, many took clerical jobs, freeing men for combat assignments.

While soldiers returning from World War I marched through a triumphal arch at the Alamo, these returning from World War II got a welcoming parade along the city's recently-completed San Antonio River Walk.

the 30th Women's Army Auxiliary Corps Post Headquarters Company disembarked from a troop train for duty at Fort Sam Houston in mid-December 1942, local Army officials expected a mediocre showing. The consensus was that "they will not make a good impression while disheveled," wrote a recruiting officer, Lt. Charlee Kelly.

The men were wrong.

"You would have been proud . . . if you had been standing there when they got off the train," Lieutenant Kelly reported. "Their noses were powdered, their shoes were shined, they showed that they were well-trained and well disciplined. Before the last ones had got off the train, the cannon was fired for retreat. Like one woman they came to attention and saluted. . . . The salutes so impressed the photographers that they stopped taking pictures and faced the flag."

By 1943, many basic jobs at Fort Sam Houston were being filled by an even more unanticipated element—prisoners of war. To keep prisoners away from strategic cities and industries, of the 511 camps in the nation 340 were in the South and Southwest, 120 of them in Texas, where 79,000 prisoners were housed. In 1943 a prisoner-of-war camp opened at Dodd Field for 1,600 prisoners. A branch camp at Camp Bullis brought local capacity to 3,000 prisoners.

With the end of the war in Europe in April 1945, Fort Sam Houston's Fourth Army got ready to prepare units arriving from Europe for the war in the Pacific, a task made unnecessary by the surrender of Japan. During the next year, Fort Sam Houston instead mustered out more than 500,000 soldiers.

Staying in San Antonio, however, were the remains of 144 German, Japanese, Austrian and Italian prisoners of war who had died. They were buried with full military honors at the Fort Sam Houston National Cemetery at the eastern edge of the post. The Germans, in line with wartime protocol, got swastikas on their tombstones.

San Antonio's first national cemetery was established just east of downtown in 1867. Its 5,000 graves include those of Gen. John Bullis, Lt. George E. M. Kelly, Congressman Harry Wurzbach—also memorialized in the name of Harry Wurzbach Road, the segment

Seen looking south past the Fort Sam Houston National Cemetery are the post golf course and newer housing areas.

nearest Fort Sam Houston of the old Camp Bullis-bound Military Highway—and a mass grave of 320 "unknown dead," among them 42 now known to have been "Buffalo soldiers," blacks who served on the Indian frontier after the Civil War.

The first burial was in 1926 at the new cemetery, named Fort Sam Houston National Cemetery in 1937, its 75 acres now 156. At the turn of the century it held 93,000 graves, including those of nine Medal of Honor winners. As aging American veterans were dying at the rate of more than 1,300 per day, new burials averaged 80 per week, with graveside services often scheduled just 15 minutes apart.

11. Through Korea and Vietnam

With the end of World War II, Fort Sam Houston's mission changed. Size and equipment requirements for an infantry division had enlarged, and the post was not big enough to accommodate them. Nor could improved weaponry with its greater ranges be fired at Camp Bullis unless its 27,000 acres were significantly enlarged, and that expense was prohibitive.

Other diversified headquarters and supply functions could continue, however. Facilities once occupied by troops forming a division could be used by expanding the medical training functions, for which Camp Bullis would also be useful. In 1946 the Medical Field Service School was moved to Fort Sam Houston from Carlisle Barracks, Pennsylvania, and other field medical units were added.

That year, the Institute of Surgical Research—established in New York City in 1943—was relocated to Brooke General Hospital. The

Robert G. Cole Junior-Senior High School, below, was built in 1963 to serve families in the new military housing developments on Dodd Field.

The 507th Air Ambulance Company pioneered techniques to airlift civilian traffic victims to nearby military and civilian hospitals.

Fort Sam Houston hosted the United States Modern Pentathlon Training Center for 30 years, beginning in 1955, the five areas of mastery for soldiers including horsemanship. Below, Capt. Edward Carfagno leads penthalon riders at the opening of the eighth annual Fort Sam Houston Horse Show in 1969.

thrust of research into trauma surgery and the potential of new antibiotic medicines had shifted with the advent of nuclear warfare, and research was needed in the care and treatment of injury from nuclear explosions. The institute's Burn Center, created in 1949 at Brooke General Hospital—by then renamed Brooke Army Medical Center—first earned worldwide renown for research on improved wound dressing that resulted in the development of skin grafting.

In January 1946 command of the Fourth Army at Fort Sam Houston went to Gen. Jonathan Wainwright, 63, whose leadership of the defense of the Pacific island of Bataan in the first three months of World War II enabled General MacArthur's main force to retreat and

The appeal of new missile technology is shown in Fort Sam Houston's 1958 Fiesta parade float, above, and in the 1964 display installation of a Redstone missile near the Quadrangle.

regroup. During his imprisonment by the Japanese, Wainwright had feared a court-martial for having surrendered. Instead, he was promoted from lieutenant general to general, presented the Medal of Honor and given a seat of honor aboard the battleship *Missouri* at the formal surrender of the Japanese.

Wainwright retired in 1947 and was replaced as Fourth Army commander by Gen. Thomas T. Handy, who had played a key behind-the-scenes role in World War II as the assistant chief of staff in the Pentagon. He left two years later to command the Army in Europe.

When the Korean War broke out in 1950, a reception center on Infantry Post processed draftees and recruits, while the Medical Field Service School increased its training and Brooke Army Medical Center began treating some 5,000 wounded soldiers.

The Medical Field Service School's most famous alumni are fictional—Col. Sherman Potter and "Hawkeye" Pierce, doctors in the long-running television series *M*A*S*H*. According to the story line, both characters had passed through the portals of Fort Sam Houston. In one episode, Colonel Potter speaks fondly of his early days as a cavalry boy at the Quadrangle before beginning his career as a doctor.

A small horse population reappeared at Fort Sam Houston in 1955, when Artillery Post stables for 30 horses were set up for the United States Modern Pentathlon Training Center. Jointly funded by the Army and a civilian nonprofit organization, the center moved from the U.S. Military Academy at West Point, where it had been housed since its inception in 1912. San Antonio's milder climate gave Pentathletes the opportunity to train year-round.

To orient medical personnel to the Vietnam combat environment, a "Republic of Vietnam Village" was set up at Camp Bullis.

The concept had originated in ancient Greece, where Spartans, looking down on the Olympic games as mere sporting events of little merit for the soldier, devised five games stressing mastery of elements considered essential for the successful soldier: broad jumping, javelin throwing, running, discus throwing and wrestling. These were updated for the modern Olympics in 1912 as the Modern Pentathlon: horseback riding, over a 600-meter course on an unfamiliar horse; pistol shooting at a turning target; swimming 300 meters; fencing; and cross-country running.

In 1977 Fort Sam Houston hosted the Modern Pentathlon World Championships that included, for the first time, women's competition. The United States took firsts in Women's Team and Individual scores. Two years later came the first sweep of all five events by a team trained at Fort Sam Houston. In the world championships held in Budapest, Hungary, Robert Nieman took the individual gold medal, while the U.S. team took the Team Gold Medal. Army support of the Modern Pentathlon ended in 1985.

Among the first American military units sent to Vietnam—in May 1962—was the 178th Signal Company from Fort Sam Houston, soon followed by 12 medical units and thousands of trainees.

In 1966 exercises at Camp Bullis, members of the 45th Surgical Hospital, top, await return of a helicopter, while, below, a Chinook CH-47 helicopter successfully lifts 8,300 pounds of sand to test its capacity for lifting a similar weight of hospital equipment.

Vietnam era Medical training peaked in 1967 when 29,000 graduated from the Medical Training Center, among them conscientious objectors trained in a Modified Basic Training Course on Infantry Post to become medics rather than combat soldiers. Brooke Army Medical Center established a satellite Burn Center in Japan, bringing quick treatment for chemical and flash burns much closer to the victims.

During these years, housing and facilities for soldiers and their families were expanding. Additional housing was added with construction in 1948 of 18 units on the old Infantry Post parade field and, two years later, of 215 duplexes and 70 single family units for officers and noncommissioned officers on Dodd Field. The complex was modeled after the winding streets and ranch-style homes typifying postwar suburban development.

First called Sam Houston Village, in 1961 it was renamed Watkins Terrace in memory of M.Sgt. Travis E. Watkins, an infantryman and Medal of Honor winner killed in action during the Korean War. At that time the nearby Sam Houston Village, built in 1953, was named Harris Heights to honor Lt. James L. Harris, a tank commander and Medal of Honor winner killed during World War II.

To serve the increasing number of families, a junior-senior high school was built in 1963 and named in honor of Lt. Col. Robert G. Cole, who was born in Fort Sam Houston's station hospital and received the Medal of Honor in 1944 shortly before his death in combat in Europe.

After Lyndon Johnson became president in 1963, a President's Suite was created on the seventh floor of Brooke Army Medical Center's main hospital, less than an hour away by helicopter from the Summer White House—Johnson's ranch home some 60 miles north of San Antonio—to meet any medical emergency of the military's new commander-in-chief.

In 1970, techniques for medical evacuation by helicopter that had been developed at Brooke Army Medical Center were adapted

During filming of the movie *The Alamo* in 1960, actor John Wayne visited patients at Brooke Army Medical Center.

by the Army for civilian traffic accident emergencies as Military Assistance to Safety and Traffic (MAST), conducted by the 507th Air Ambulance Company from Fort Sam Houston's Charles L. Kelly Heliport. The MAST program, which spread nationwide, was eventually succeeded by civilian helicopter operations.

12. The Cold War's End and Beyond

As the war in Vietnam wound down, American military consolidation brought the merger in 1971 of the two Army commands in the central United States—the Fifth Army, headquartered at Fort Sheridan near Chicago, and the Fourth Army, headquartered in Fort Sam Houston's Quadrangle, a change designed to save the Army $11 million annually. The enlarged surviving Fifth Army gained combined jurisdiction over a 13-state area from the Canadian to the Mexican border.

Outside the Quadrangle, the medical training mission that had dominated the rest of the post since the close of World War II expanded. Fragmented Army medical services were consolidated in a new entity known as the U.S. Army Health Services Command, brought together at Fort Sam Houston in 1973 under Maj. Gen. Spurgeon H. Neel Jr.

A major medical services component was already located at Fort Sam Houston—the Army's Medical Training Center, which up to that point had trained 300,000 military medics. That summer it became part of the Academy of Health Sciences as it moved from its quarters in a cluster of World War II era frame buildings into a new nearby headquarters complex complete with classrooms, a dining

In 1971 Quadrangle ceremonies marking the merger of the Fourth Army into the Fifth Army, Lt. Gen. George Underwood Jr., left, Fourth Army commander, takes the Fourth Army colors from his top noncommissioned officer, Command Sgt. Maj. Robert Eckenrod Jr., to prepare for retiring the flag.

The U.S. Army Health Services Command, its headquarters no longer reached through the Spanish Colonial Revival New Post entrance below, moved in 1973 into the new complex above, soon surrounded by clusters of 32 low-rise barracks buildings.

hall and what grew into a grouping of 32 three-story barracks buildings.

As consolidation continued with the end of the Cold War with the Soviet Union, in 1991 the Academy of Health Sciences became part of the Fort Sam Houston–based Army Medical Department Center and School, which included Army medical schools elsewhere. The Health Services Command itself was reorganized in 1994 as the U.S. Army Medical Command, employing 27,500 military personnel and 24,000 civilians in training centers and at eight Army medical centers throughout the United States.

Fifty years after opening of New Post's Brooke General Hospital, in the fall of 1987 ground was broken for a replacement facility in an undeveloped expanse at the southeast corner of Fort Sam Houston near the intersection of interstates 35 and 410. It opened in the spring of 1996. Its 450-bed capacity can be expanded to 650 beds.

Although medical training and care continued to dominate activities, Fort Sam Houston remains useful for annual training exercises for Regular Army and reserve troops on post and at Camp Bullis, maintaining readiness for periodic deployments during international crises. In 1990's Operation Desert Storm, for example, Fort Sam Houston's 41st Combat Support Hospital and its 507th Medical Air Ambulance Company went to Saudi Arabia, while 27 Texas, Oklahoma and California Fifth Army National Guard units were mobilized at Fort Sam Houston and also sent overseas.

Effects of the terrorist attacks of Sept. 11, 2001, had an instant impact on the post. Throughout its history it had remained unusual as an open post, bisected by an unfenced public highway—North New Braunfels Avenue—that allowed vehicles unrestricted access down intersecting streets.

Two medics training under chemical and biological warfare conditions in 1978 take a break outside a field hospital at Camp Bullis, where students, below, receive outdoor instruction.

As the military went into heightened readiness, however, all but a few of the 26 entrances onto the post were closed. Concrete barriers and spools of razor wire blocked the suddenly locked gates at both ends of North New Braunfels Avenue. At the entrances, newly posted guards implemented strict identification procedures. Once procedures were standardized, properly-identified civilian visitors were once again admitted through the Walters Street entrance.

Within the Quadrangle, descendants of deer housed there for a century had become skittish in the absence of visitors, but they relaxed and became tamer once tourists returned.

The broad parade grounds and ordered groups of distinctive buildings—representing all major types of military construction since the Civil War—had made Fort Sam Houston a tourist attraction since its beginnings. As deterioration of these buildings accelerated in the 1960s and questions of their fate arose, appreciation of their significance heightened. In the 1960s the short-lived Fort Sam Houston Historical Society rescued the Stilwell House, the distinctive Infantry Post commander's residence once the home of World War II's Gen. Joseph W. Stilwell, from planned demolition.

In 1968 the partially restored Stilwell House was turned into a military museum. Exhibits were moved to a refurbished Artillery Post mess hall, where the Fort Sam Houston Museum opened in 1976. The museum, directed since 1978 by John Manguso, is slated to move into larger facilities.

In 1978, the private U.S. Army Medical Department Museum Foundation was formed to provide a new home for the collection of medical military artifacts housed in the school's basement since the Medical Field Service School came to Fort Sam Houston 22 years earlier. The collection moved nearby in 1989 into the first section of a $9 million, 40,000-square-foot building museum building completed in 2001. Operated by the Army and directed by Tom McMasters, the museum includes covered outdoor displays.

Continued preservation of the Stillwell House became a founding goal in 1984 of the Society for the Preservation of Historic Fort

The Towers, a retirement complex built by USAA on Harry Wurzbach Highway just outside Fort Sam Houston, rises above the U.S. Army Medical Department Museum.

Sam Houston, its activities buoyed by the growing preservation movement in the city beyond. Already efforts of the civilian community—led in large part by the San Antonio Conservation Society—had culminated, in 1975, with designation of the Quadrangle and Staff, Infantry and Cavalry and Light Artillery posts as National Historical Landmarks. Three landmarks were also listed individually in the National Register of Historic Places—the Quadrangle, Pershing House and Gift Chapel.

By 1991, a $270,000 grant from the Department of Defense Legacy Resource Management Program resulted in a study and formal agreement on management of the post's cultural and historical resources among five groups: the Department of the Army, President's Advisory Council on Historic Preservation, Texas Historical Commission, City of San Antonio and San Antonio Conservation Society. The official inventory listed 934 historic structures at Fort Sam Houston, far more than at the venerable U.S. Military Academy at West Point and nine times as many as at Colonial Williamsburg.

A general $100.3 million construction program including restoration of active facilities on post began in 1992. Interiors and exteriors of historic structures were repaired and restored, and many temporary buildings were removed, among them a sprawling World War

The Fort Sam Houston Museum, which opened in the Stilwell House in 1968, reopened in 1976 in a refurbished Artillery Post mess hall, right. The museum is slated for larger quarters.

Highlighting 1990s construction at Fort Sam Houston was the new Brooke Army Medical Center, above, which opened in 1996.

II–era warehouse complex east of North New Braunfels Avenue. Other projects included refurbishing and enlarging the Post Exchange and building a new Commissary. In recognition of the Army's role in enhancing the post's historic resources as part of all this, in 1993 Fifth Army Commander Lt. Gen. Tom Jaco received the Texas Historical Commission's Texas Award for Historic Preservation.

At the beginning of the 21st century, such work continues—among it a second major restoration of the Gift Chapel—as more

The sally port entry to Fort Sam Houston's historic Quadrangle has changed little in more than a century and a quarter.

ABOVE: BROOKE ARMY MEDICAL CENTER
BELOW: FORT SAM HOUSTON MUSEUM

This sculpture honoring combat medics is near the entrance of the U.S. Army Medical Department Museum.

than 10,000 permanent party Army personnel and 5,000 civilian employees report for ongoing duty at Fort Sam Houston, generating $3 billion a year for the San Antonio economy. At the "home of Army medicine," 30,000 military medical personnel are trained each year on the 3,000-acre post and on the 27,000-acre Camp Bullis in northwestern Bexar County.

An expansion in Fort Sam Houston's role came in September 2002, when former Brooke Army Medical Center facilities—vacated for the newer hospital complex—were selected to become the headquarters for U.S. Army South. Previously headquartered at Fort Buchanan in Puerto Rico, U.S. Army South oversees Army and National Guard operations in Central and South America and the Caribbean, in addition to training foreign military forces and coordinating operations with the region's 32 countries. The move added some 300 military and civilian personnel at Fort Sam Houston.

Preservation of the historic medical complex while renovating its facilities for modern use continued the evolution of the core of Fort Sam Houston into a living museum. Generals still pass daily through the stone-walled Quadrangle's sally port to their offices above. Colonels and their families still live in Staff Post's stately columned quarters on one side of the parade grounds, while across the way the rows of two-story red and buff-colored brick barracks buildings still seem to hold enlisted men ready to file out into formation for firing of the sunset gun.

Those barracks are now quiet at night, however, for closer inspection reveals them to be military offices open during daytime hours only. And the sunset gun that sounds nightly is now only a recording, broadcast, as is the bugle call of taps, electronically.

Fort Sam Houston still serves a growing host of contemporary functions as one of the nation's major military installations, even as its distinguished past pervades its grounds.

Selected Bibliography

Cagle, Eldon, Jr. *Quadrangle: The History of Fort Sam Houston.* Austin: Eakin Press, 1985.

David, Lester, and Irene David. *Ike and Mamie, The Story of the General and His Lady.* New York: G. P. Putnam, 1981.

Davis, Burke. *The Billy Mitchell Story.* Philadelphia: Chilton Books Co., 1969.

Downey, Fairfax. *Indian-Fighting Army.* New York: Charles Scribners Sons, 1941.

Field, William T., comp. *The Chinese Texans.* San Antonio: The Institute of Texan Cultures of the University of Texas at San Antonio, 1981.

Fisher, Lewis F. *Eyes Right! A Vintage Postcard Profile of San Antonio's Military.* San Antonio: Maverick Publishing Co., 2000.

_____. *San Antonio: Outpost of Empires.* San Antonio: Maverick Publishing Co., 1997.

_____. *Saving San Antonio: The Precarious Preservation of a Heritage.* Lubbock: Texas Tech University Press, 1996.

Foulois, Benjamin D., and C. V. Glines. *From the Wright Brothers to the Astronauts: The Memoirs of Major General Benjamin D. Foulois.* New York: McGraw-Hill, 1968.

Freeman, Douglas Southall. *R. E. Lee, A Biography.* Vol. 1. New York: Charles Scribner's Sons, 1962.

Goldhurst, Richard. *Pipe Clay and Drill: John J. Pershing, The Classic American Soldier.* New York: Reader's Digest Press, 1977.

Handy, Mary. *History of Fort Sam Houston.* San Antonio: Naylor Press, 1950.

Hatch, Alden. *Red Carpet for Mamie.* New York: Henry Holt & Co., 1954.

Haynes, Robert V. *A Night of Violence: The Houston Riot of 1917.* Baton Rouge: Louisiana State University Press, 1976.

Hurley, Alfred F. *Billy Mitchell: Crusader for Air Power.* New York: Franklin Watts Inc., 1964.

Johns, E. B., comp. *Camp Travis and Its Part in the World War.* New York: Wynkoop, Hallenbeck, Crawford Co., 1918.

Manchester, William. *American Caesar—Douglas MacArthur, 1880–1964.* New York: Dell Publishing Co., 1978.

Manguso, John M. *A Pocket Guide to the Cavalry and Light Artillery Post, Fort Sam Houston, Texas.* San Antonio: Fort Sam Houston Museum, 1994.

_____. *A Pocket Guide to Historic Fort Sam Houston.* San Antonio: Fort Sam Houston Museum, 2000.

_____. *A Pocket Guide to the New Post, Fort Sam Houston, Texas.* San Antonio: Fort Sam Houston Museum, 1995.

_____. *A Pocket Guide to the Staff Post, Fort Sam Houston.* San Antonio: Fort Sam Houston Museum, 1991.

_____. *Fort Sam in the Big War, 1940–45.* San Antonio: Fort Sam Houston Museum, 1995.

_____. *Surrounded by History: How Fort Sam Houston's Built Environ-*

ment Embodies the Values of Distinguished Soldiers. San Antonio: Fort Sam Houston Museum, 1999.

Mayhall, Mildred P. *Indian Wars of Texas.* Waco: Texian Press, 1965.

_____. *The Kiowas.* Norman: University of Oklahoma Press, 1963.

Minton, John, ed. *The Houston Riot and Courts-Martial of 1917.* San Antonio: Carver Cultural Center in cooperation with the University of Texas Institute of Texan Cultures at San Antonio, n.d.

Nimitz, Chester W. *Some Thoughts to Live By.* Fredericksburg, Tex.: Admiral Nimitz Foundation, 1981.

Richardson, Rupert N., et al. *Frontier Forts of Texas.* Waco: Texian Press, 1966.

Rogers, Geraldine, and Susan Ewick. *St. Paul's Episcopal Church in San Antonio.* San Antonio: N.p., 1995.

Roosevelt, Theodore. *The Rough Riders.* New York: Scribner's, 1899.

Ruiz, Ramon Eduardo. *The Great Rebellion—Mexico, 1905–1924.* New York: W. W. Norton & Co. 1980.

Smythe, Donald. *Guerilla Warrior, The Early Life of John J. Pershing.* New York: Charles Scribner's Sons, 1973.

Thompson, Frank. *Texas Hollywood: Filmmaking in San Antonio since 1911.* San Antonio: Maverick Publishing Co., 2002.

Treadwell, Mattie E. *The Women's Army Corps* in *The United States Army in World War II, Special Studies.* Washington, D.C.: Department of the Army Office of Military History, 1954.

Turner, Leo. *The Story of Fort Sam Houston, 1876–1936.* San Antonio: N. p., 1936.

Tyler, Ron, ed. *The New Handbook of Texas.* 6 vols. Austin: The Texas State Historical Association, 1996.

Woolford, Sam and Bess. *The San Antonio Story.* San Antonio: Naylor Co., 1963.

Acknowledgments

A special thank you goes to John Manguso, director of the Fort Sam Houston Museum. John is a living encyclopedia of Fort Sam Houston history. His encouragement, guidance and review of the drafts have been of great value. Museum staff members Jackie Davis and Martin Callahan have also been helpful.

Tom Shelton, photo archivist at the University of Texas at San Antonio Institute of Texan Cultures, and a fellow student and friend when we attended Trinity University, has been helpful in photo research. Hazel Stitt at the Dwight D. Eisenhower Library in Abilene, Kansas, came up with an appropriate photograph of President Eisenhower. My wife, Carolyn Ann Cagle, lent important help, encouragement and support.

I am also grateful to Maverick Publishing's Lewis F. Fisher for editing and revising the manuscript, expanding the photo search and providing captions.

Index